I Felt A Bit Funny

ACKNOWLEDGMENTS

I would like to thank Chris for all his support and assistance in the development and writing of this book; my daughters for their kind assistance, and Ben Hobday for his wonderful patience and knowledge of computers.

I Felt A Bit Funny

Create crazy caricatures from needle-felted wool

Carol Rowan

NEW
HOLLAND

Contents

Introduction

I have always loved craft. When my daughter suggested I try needle felting I was surprised to find just how few materials were needed to get started. I purchased a foam pad, a packet of pipe cleaners (chenille sticks), some felting needles and some sheep's wool, and couldn't wait to begin. For me, the bright colours and organic and wholesome feel of the wool added to its appeal. Cute little animals began to take shape in my hands and soon I began to make 'human' caricature creations. Mostly the wool is shaped by rolling it into balls or oblongs. The more figures I made, the more confident I became. I found that my beginner's mistakes were easily rectified. A too large shape was, by constant needling, made smaller. I added more wool if I wasn't happy with my results, though I did discover that you need to use the right wool and needles.

I showed my creations to a craft shop owner and she put them in the window of her store. To my surprise they sold.

The wonderful thing about wool felting is that each figure you make is your own unique creation; and no two figures that you make are ever completely alike. Each figure is, in effect, a wool sculpture in which the wool is manipulated to create identifying characteristics. You don't need to make every detail accurate, just choose those features that are distinct for your purpose, such as a heavy brow, a posture or a profession, and each one comes to life.

Materials

Wool

When I first began felting, I invested in an assortment of colours of merino wool. The needle-felting guide I had said merely to use wool, and in my ignorance I didn't know there were many different types. The figures I made were hard to shape and the needle marks were clearly visible. It was only by trial and error that I discovered my mistake; merino wool is very fine, and its fibres are silky, soft and slippery, which makes it an inappropriate choice for needle felting figures. The best wools to use are the coarser types, Border Leicester or Romney, for example, although sometimes these can be hard to source. The figures in this book have been made using readily available carded New Zealand wool.

Most wool on the market is either combed or carded. The combed process makes the fibres of the wool longer. This type of wool is usually sold in a twisted, long, rope-like bundle often called a top or roving. I occasionally use combed wool for hairstyles. Carded wool is easy to felt as its fibres are naturally more tangled. Another wool I've tried recently is alpaca. It is excellent for forming realistic hair.

Never cut the wool that you are using. If the wool is cut, it is very difficult to felt as the wool fibres become too short. Instead, always pull it apart. Take hold of the wool rope with both hands and gently pull it until it comes apart. If the wool resists and you find it too hard, just adjust your hands. It becomes easy with practise. Carded wool, on the other hand, is far easier to handle. Just grab an amount, and it will pull away easily.

Above: The top 6 rolls of wool are all examples of New Zealand carded wool The single roll in orange in the middle at the bottom is an example of merino wool. Note the difference in the sheen on the merino wool.

Tools

Needles

Sculpting with felt requires a specific type of
needle. Unlike standard sewing needles, a felting
needle has barbs along its shaft that catches, matts
and tangles the woollen fibres when it is moved
in and out, or 'needles' the loose wool. It is the
constant stabbing movement of the needle through
the wool that binds it into the fibrous mass that
we call felt. The more you stab, the firmer the felt
becomes.

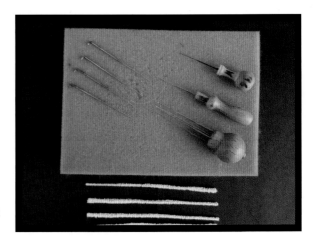

*Above: Single dry felting needles, foam/
sponge felting pad, and pipe cleaners.*

There are three different types of felting needle: Crown, Star and Triangular. The crown
needle has one line of barbs close to the needle's tip and is useful for fine work. The star needle
has more barbs that reach a third of the way up the needle-point and can be used for general
felting. The triangular needle has the greatest number of barbs spread up the needle-point. It is
my needle of choice and using it makes the felting process quicker and easier.

The three most common sizes of needles are 40, 38 and 36, with 40 being the finest and best
for fine detail. Sizes 38 and 36 can be used for general work. I prefer working with a size 38 needle
as it slides effortlessly into any hard matted felt shape. Please do be aware that these needles are
sharp and care should be taken not to leave them lying around.

Needle holder

Holding the felting needle in your hand is recommended by some needle-felting tutors, but I find this uncomfortable and instead prefer to hold my needle within a needle holder. Needle holders are specially designed for felting and can hold more than one needle at a time, meaning you can felt the work more quickly. I mainly work with a single needle but will use a 4-prong needle holder when felting larger clumps of wool for speed, and even a 6-needle holder for making a flat piece of felt to be used, for example, as a skirt.

In this book I have used the triangular 38 gauge dry felting needle for all projects unless stated otherwise.

Brushes

There are two recommended surfaces for needle-felting a piece of wool into a flat shape. The first is a brush (see picture). A brush is an excellent surface for small pieces of work. On the downside, I've sometimes found that the wool I use may stick in the bristles making it hard to remove a piece of work without spoiling its shape. Also, just a little bit of over-energetic needling can end up breaking the tip of a needle.

The other surface I like to use for needle-felting is the foam pad. Foam pads are larger than brushes and therefore better surfaces for felting large shapes. Foam will wear out quicker than a brush and will need to be replaced regularly. To extend the life of your foam move the felt around the pad when you work it into shapes so that it doesn't become too worn in one place. When purchasing a foam pad, choose a high-density foam from a craft supplier rather than using upholstery foam, which breaks down much more quickly.

Pipe Cleaners/Chenille Stems

Although felted figures are quite firm, I like to be able to set mine in poses. I have found that the figures are far more pliable and poseable if they are made with a pipe cleaner framework. I have worked with chenille stems and pipe cleaners from craft shops, and have found that those designed to be safe for very young children are not strong enough to hold the weight of the felt figures. As I don't want my figures to look like slumped rag dolls, I had to go in search of the fast-disappearing tobacconist shops to purchase the original pipe cleaners. These are made with stronger wire as they are designed to be pushed through a pipe's stem. They are available to purchase on the internet. All figures in this book have been made using pipe cleaners that are 16 cm (6½ in) long.

Techniques

Using Felting Needles

Needles can be purchased with or without their respective needle holders. Replacing a broken needle or inserting a needle into a holder is usually a very simple task. There are many brands available so always refer to the manufacturer's instructions. Take the needle in your hand in a way that is most comfortable to you. I find the best way is between my thumb and index finger. The needle should always be held straight as it enters and leaves the wool. Using a backward and forward motion, slowly push and pull your needle in and out of your wool shape, taking care not to push the needle too far through the shape as you don't want to prick your fingers. Also, take care not to bend the needle when it is inside the felt in case the needle snaps.

You can either hold your wool shape in your hands while felting it or place it on the foam pad. If you find it easier to hold your piece in your hand while needling, be very careful of stabbing your fingers. I realise that I become clumsier when I'm growing tired. If you constantly prick your fingers, take a tea or coffee break.

Shaping the Wool

To make felt figures the only shaping that you will do is to roll felt into balls for the head, bosoms and bottoms. To do this, take a handful of wool and fold in the edges before rolling it with your fingers into a tight ball. Using short stabbing movements needle your wool until the ball is firm. When you think your ball is firm enough test it by squeezing it between your fingers. If it squashes it's not ready. You must continue needling until it's hard and does not give when squeezed. The needling process to get your wool into a firm ball is one of the most time consuming of making figures. The felt needs to be firm; for example, if the head isn't tight enough, the face will not look right. The good thing about needle felting is that you can always add more wool to get your desired shape. If you find you have added too much wool, then constant needling will reduce its size.

For the rest of the figure you will be using a pipe cleaner framework as the basis for the shape, wrapping the wool around the frame before needling it into place. Use small pieces of wool to build up your shape. Large pieces, when wrapped, can be lumpy and bulky, requiring more time needling them into shape.

Below is a rough guide to the sizes of wool I mention in the instructions to each figure. These measurements may vary slightly depending on the wool you use. You will find that the wool is very springy and the thickness of these pieces will vary.

Wisp: 1 x 3 cm (3/8 x 1¼ in) (Please note, this is a very thin, only a few strands of wool).

Small piece: 3 x 5 cm (1¼ x 2 in)

Piece: 5 x 10 cm (2 x 4 in)

Clump: 8 x 14 cm (3¼ x 5½ in)

Handful: 8 x 20 cm (3¼ x 8 in)

When you start to make clothes, you will need to place the wool onto a foam pad, arrange it in the desired shape and, needle it so that it is flat, then carefully turn the piece over before needling the other side. This method makes a piece of felt similar to commercial felt. Wrap the shape around your figure and needle it into place. The templates provided are good guidelines to use for the clothes required.

Making a
Felted Figure

Making the Head

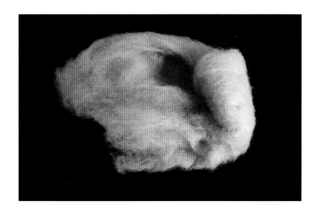

1) Take a handful of flesh-coloured wool and fold the edges in until you have a ball.

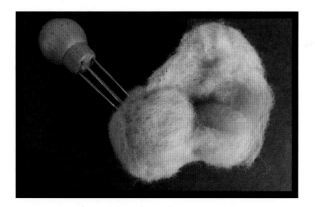

2) Needle with a single or four-needle holder until the ball is firm and keeps its shape.

3) Continue to add more pieces of wool until you have a solid ball approximately 5 cm (2 in) in diameter. If you squeeze the ball between your fingers it should have very little give. If you can still squash it, then it needs more wool and work.

 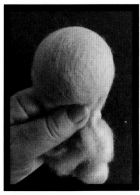

4) Take a clump of flesh-coloured wool, flatten it in your fingers before placing the ball in its centre. Fold the wool tightly around the ball.

Forming the Neck and Body

1) Take a 16 cm (6½ in) pipe cleaner and wrap it tightly around the base of the head. The ends of the pipe cleaner at each side of the head should be of equal length. These wires form the base of the arms.

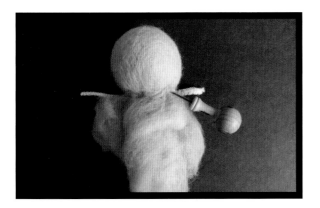

2) Needle the excess wool around the pipe cleaner a little, covering it at the neck and forming a chin.

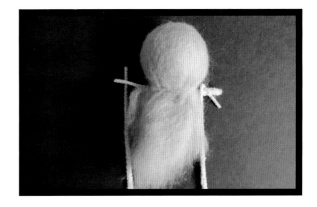

3) Place a pipe cleaner vertically 2.5 cm (1 in) from the centre of the neck, projecting 2 cm (¾ in) above the right arm. Wrap the short end around the arm three times

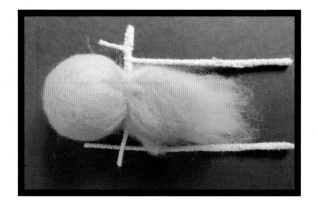

4) When the join is firm and tight repeat on the left side.

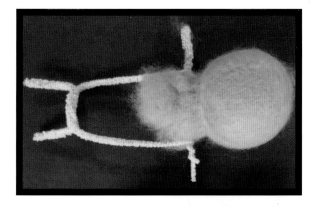

6) Straighten the ends to make the start of the legs, these should measure approximately 3 cm (1¼ in).

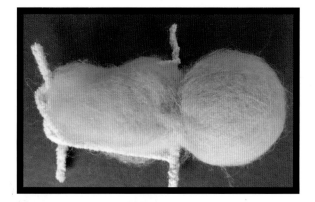

5) Measure 8 cm (3⅛ in) from the join. Bend the vertical pipe cleaners at that point in toward each other. Without pulling the pipe cleaners too tight, cross one pipe cleaner over the other.

Forming the Legs and Feet

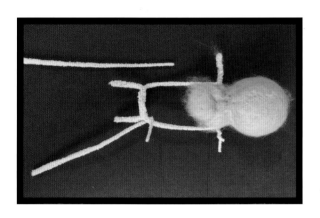

2) Wrap the hook three times around the framework at the base of the body. Then wrap the original 3 cm (1¼ in) of leg around the joint to make it firm and strong. Repeat on the other side. Make sure both legs are the same length.

1) To form a leg, place another pipe cleaner at the base of the framework. Hook it over the twisted framework base and place it at one side. The 'hook' should project 2 cm (¾ in) over the framework.

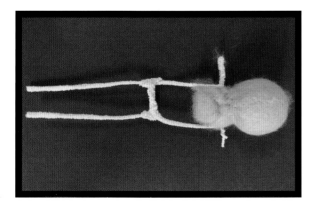

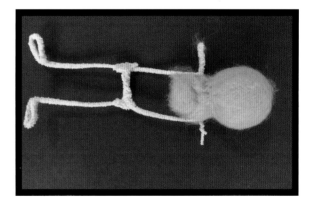

3) To form the feet, bend each leg 10 cm (4 in) from the lower body framework. Fold a foot in half. It should be approximately 2 cm (¾ in) long. Repeat for the other foot.

Padding the Framework

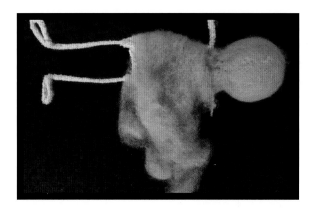

1) Take a handful of flesh-coloured wool and begin wrapping it around the body.

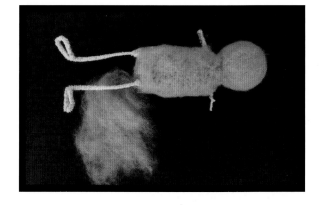

3) Take a clump of flesh-coloured wool and begin to wrap it tightly around the first leg.

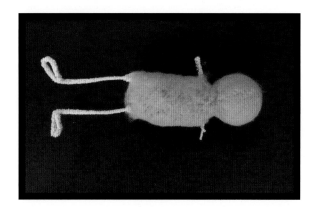

2) Continue to wrap wool around the body until it is firm, adding more wool as needed. Needle it into shape until the body is firm.

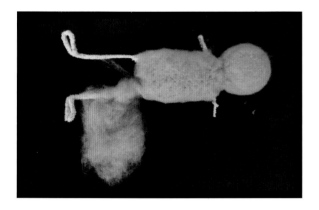

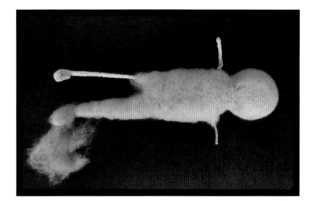

4) Continue adding wool and wrapping until the leg is the right shape and then needle the wool until it is firm.

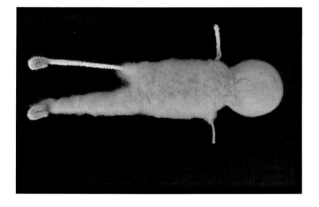

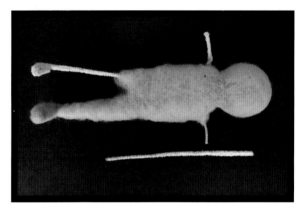

6) Fold back onto the foot any wool left hanging over the end. Add small pieces of wool to the ankle joint and foot until you are satisfied with the result. Needle in place.

5) Take a small piece of flesh-coloured wool and begin to wrap it tightly around the foot.

Forming the Arms and Hands

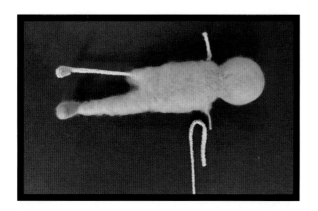

1) Bend a pipe cleaner 5 cm (2 in) from one end.

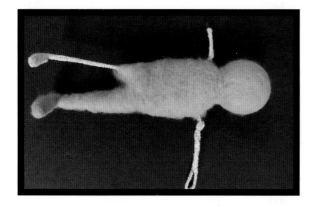

2) Place the bend 2.5 cm (1 in) from the end of the arm. Bend the arm framework up and wrap it tightly around the new pipe cleaner arm making a firm joint.

3) Form a hand by bending the pipe cleaner 1.5 cm (1½ in) at the end.

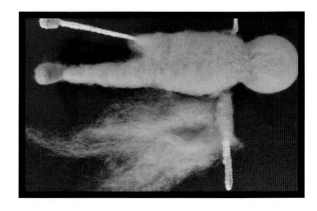

4) Take a clump of flesh-coloured wool and wrap it tightly around the arm. When satisfied with the shape and thickness, needle felt until firm.

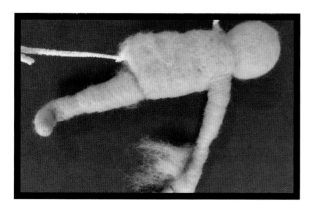

5) Take a small piece of flesh-coloured wool and wrap it around the hand, folding in any wool that hangs over the edge. Continue to add small amounts of wool until you're satisfied with the hand, wrist and shoulder.

6) Now repeat the process on the other side of the body. Needle the figure until you're satisfied with the finished result. The more you needle, the firmer the shape will become and the more wool you will use.

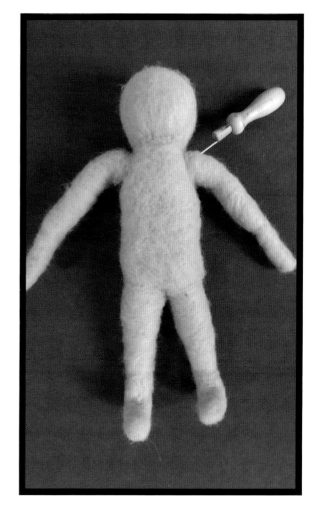

Forming Bosoms
and Bottoms

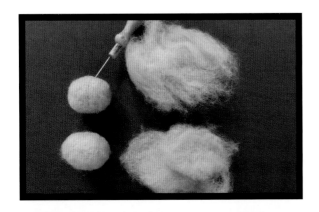

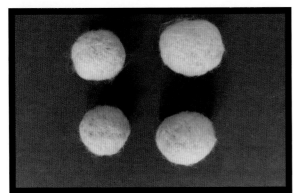

(1–1¼ in) in diameter. When making buxom seaside ladies I make their bottoms measure 3.5–4 cm (1½ in) in diameter.

2) To make the bosoms, follow the instructions above, making them 2.5–3 cm (1–1¼ in) each in diameter. If you don't want the buxom look, make them smaller.

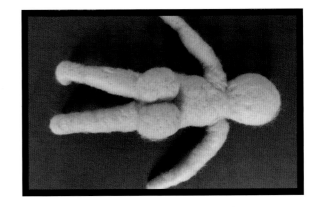

1) To make the bottom, take two clumps of flesh-coloured wool of equal size, rolling them up into balls and needling them until firm. When making a male figure, I usually make the cheeks of the bottom 2.5–3 cm

3) Needle felt the side of the bottom or bosom that you will place against the body so that it is flat.

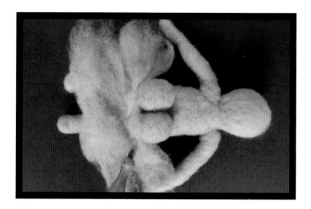

1) For the bottom, position the felt balls appropriately against the figure. Taking a handful of flesh-coloured wool, needle felt the balls and wool along the back of the legs. Fold up over the bottom.

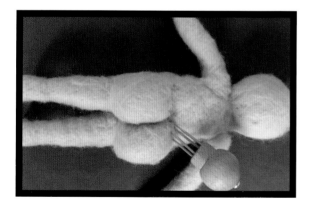

2) Needle felt the wool all around the bottom until the felt balls are firmly in place. Using a needle holder containing 4 needles will help attach them more securely.

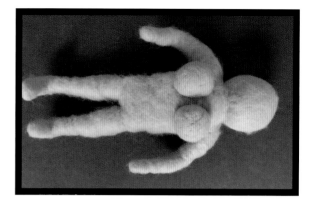

1) For the bosoms, place the shapes on the body. Take a handful of flesh-coloured wool and place it underneath the bosoms and needle into place.

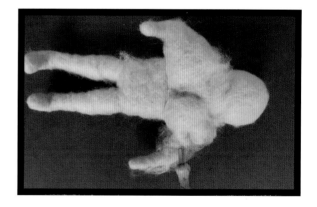

2) Bring the wool over the bosoms to hold them in place. Adjust to your own preference, then needle around the shapes until firmly in place.

Adding the Nose

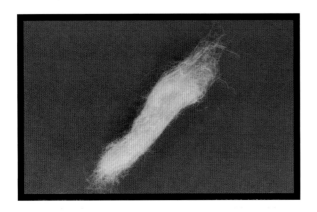

1) Take a small piece of beige wool and roll it between your fingers to a thin, long sausage shape.

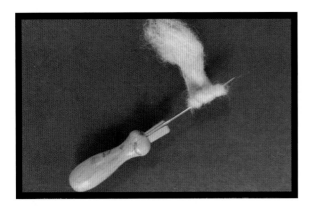

2) This is the tricky bit. Using your fingers, or a needle, begin to tightly roll up the thickest end of the sausage. Roll it about five times, until you see the pea-shaped bobble needed for the end of the nose start to take form. This method creates wispy bits on each side of the bobble that will become the nostrils. The more you roll the wool the larger the nose becomes, so make more turns if you're making a male figure.

3) Gently needle it on your pad so it will hold its shape.

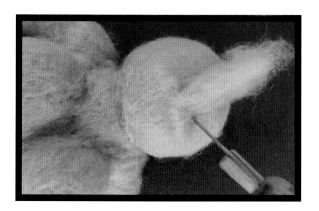

4) Position the nose on the face. Take a fine film of wool and gently needle it over the nose and onto the face to hold it in place.

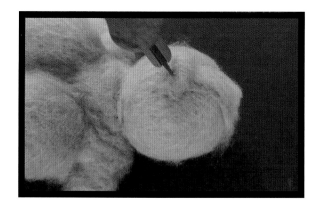

5) To make the nostril holes, gently push your needle up the nose to make an indentations in each nostril. Take care not to push your needle too far into the wool — you don't want to pierce the nose.

6) Your nose should now look similar to this.

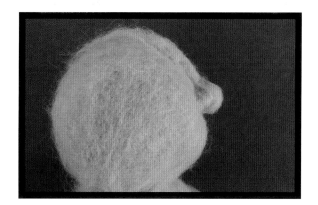

Adding the Mouth

 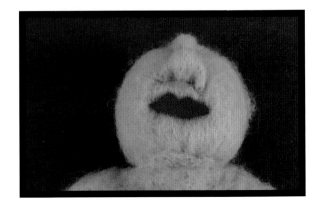

1) Take a wisp of red wool. Fold it in half
and arrange it under the nose.

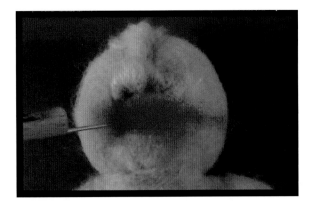

2) Begin to needle it into place while teasing
the wool into a mouth shape.

Adding the Eyes and Eyebrows

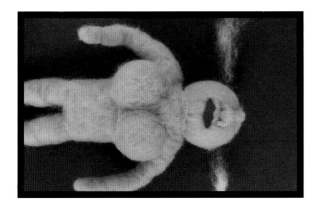

1) For the eyeball, take a small piece of white wool and roll it into a ball.

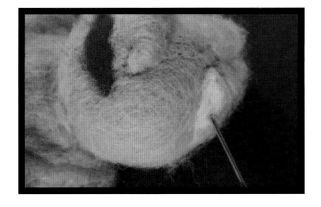

2) Place the eyeball on the face and needle it into an eye shape.

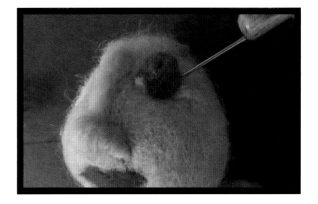

3) For the iris, take a smaller piece of coloured wool and roll it into a small ball. Place the iris in the centre of the eyeball and needle into place.

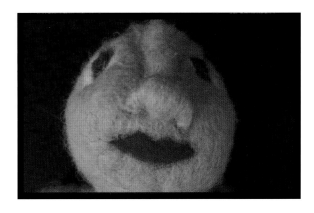

4) Repeat with the other eye. ⟶

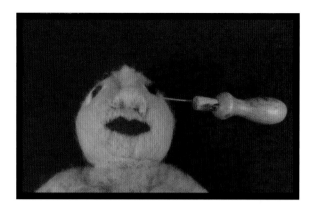

5) For the pupil, take a wisp of black wool and roll it between your fingers to make a small ball. Place in the centre of the iris and needle the pupil into place. Repeat with the other eye.

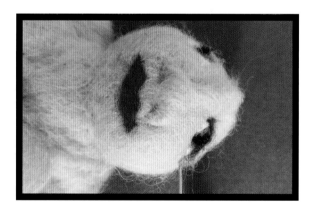

6) For the eyelash, take a wisp of brown wool and roll it into a long thin sausage. Place at one end of the eye and gently needle around the outside of the eyeball.

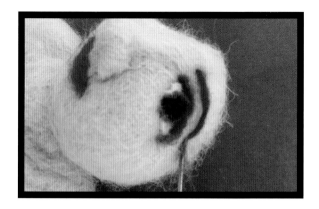

7) For the eyebrow, take a wisp of brown wool and roll it into a long thin sausage. Place at above the eye and gently needle into an arc.

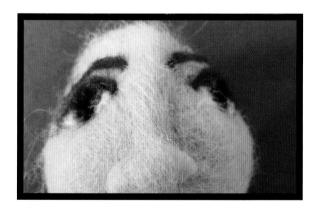

8) Repeat with other eye.

Adding the Ears

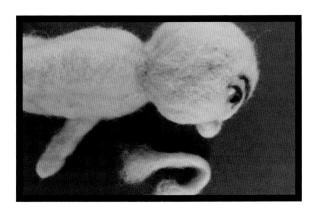

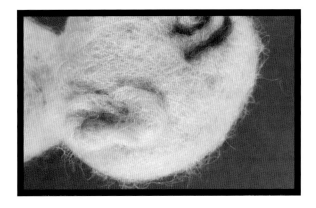

1) A figure with short hair will need ears. Take a small piece of flesh-coloured wool, roll into a sausage shape and fold over.

3) If you work the wool, the fold makes a good ear. Any surplus wool can be needled flat behind the ear.

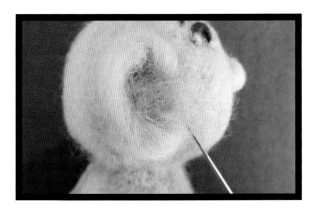

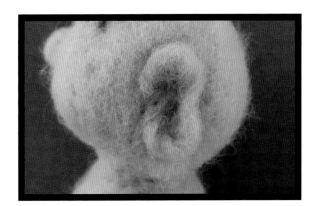

2) Needle to one side of the head at the point where the ear should be, between the eyebrow and mouth.

Adding a Moustache and Beard

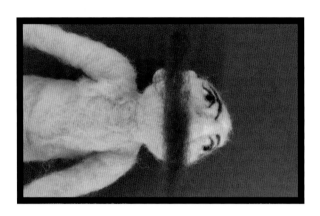

1) Take a small piece of brown wool and arrange it on the face under the nose.

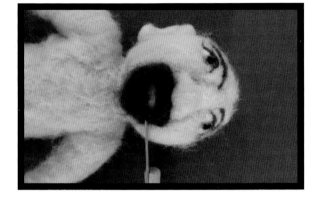

3) Add wisps of brown wool to make a beard.

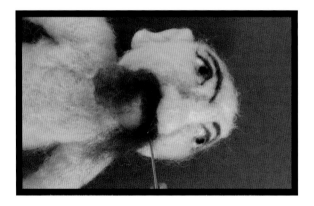

2) Needle into a moustache shape.

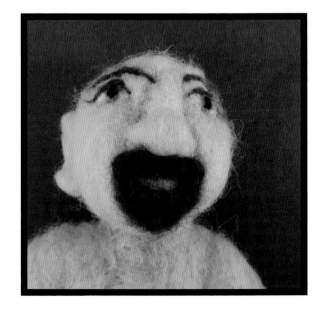

Adding the Hair

1) Take a handful of coloured wool. Arrange over the head and needle into place.

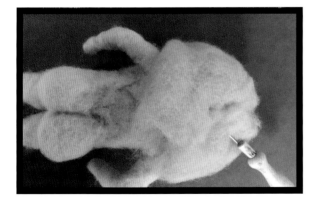

2) As you needle, decide how tight or how long you want the hair to be. The more you needle the wool, the tighter the hairstyle. Use a single needle for this

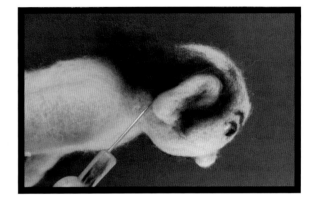

3) To make receding hair, take a piece of coloured wool and needle it around the ears and around the back of the head.

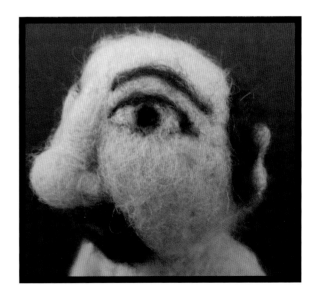

Making
Characters

Adding Clothing

Beachwear is the easiest clothing to make. A good choice for a first project.

You will need

- Needle-felted female figure, made following the instructions for Making a Felted Figure
- Coloured wool, for the bikini
- Single size 38 triangle felting needle

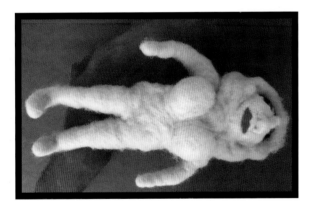

1) To make a swimsuit, take a handful of red wool and place it on the front of the figure. Needle it into the shape of a swimsuit. Needle into place.

2) Turn the figure over and add more wool as necessary.

3) Needle the wool tightly around the figure. Make sure all parts of the figure are evenly covered.

4) Bend the figure into a sitting position. Make sure that the back of the thighs are covered with wool after you have bent them.

Beach Belles

These beach belles require minimal costuming. They are also great to use up leftover wool.

Bikini Babe

You will need

- Needle-felted female figure, made following the instructions for Making a Felted Figure
- Grey wool, for the hair
- Light blue wool for the eyes and eye shadow
- Purple wool, for the bikini
- Black wool, for the pupils
- Brown wool, for the eyelids and eyebrows
- White wool, for the eyes
- Red wool, for the lips
- Single size 38 triangle felting needle

1) Make the female figure following the instructions for Making a Felted Figure. Add your choice of hair and the facial features.

2) To add eye shadow to the face, take a wisp of light blue wool and needle it between the eye and eyebrow.

3) To make the bikini pants, make a small handful of purplewool. Needle over the lower torso (being careful to leave the midriff a beige colour).

4) To make the bikini top, take a similar amount of the same colour. Roll and tease into a thin long rectangle, wrap around the bust and the figure's back. Start needling under the bust. This wool should cover most of the bust but not be too thick around the back.

5) If you want to add a trim to the bikini, take a small piece of white wool and roll it into a sausage shape that will wrap around the bikini top and needle into place.

6) Take a small piece of white wool. Roll it into a similar size and place this around the top of your bikini pants. Needle firmly into place, making sure it doesn't cover the figure's midriff.

ICE CREAM CONE
You will need

- Fawn wool, for the ice cream cone
- White wool, for the ice cream
- Red or brown wool, for the raspberry or chocolate sauce
- Single size 38 triangle felting needle

3) Take a wisp of red wool and roll it between your fingers into a long sausage. Place one end of the wisp between the cone and the cream and needle gently. Twist it around the ice cream, needling into place. Needle the cone into place attaching it to the figure's hand.

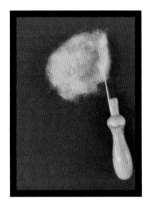 

1) Take a piece of fawn wool and roll it into a cone.

2) Needle to hold the shape then take a similar size piece of white wool and place on the cone. Needle the white wool into an ice cream cone shape.

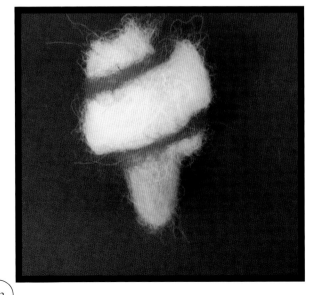

SWIMSUIT SIREN

This babe's outfit offers a great example of incorporating other materials into your project to enhance the look of the felted figure.

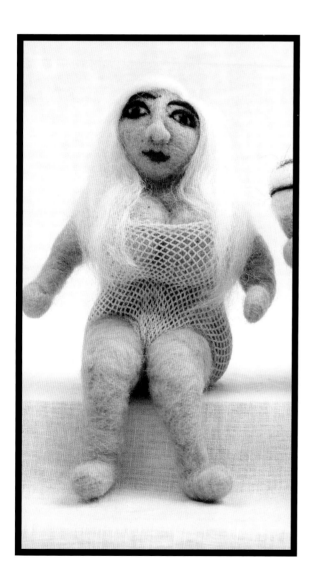

You will need

- Needle-felted female figure, made following the instructions for Making a Felted Figure
- Red wool, for the lips
- Blue wool, for the irises
- Brown wool, for the eyelids and brows
- Black wool, for the pupils
- White wool, for the eyes
- White combed merino wool, for the hair
- Coloured fishnet tights
- Sewing needle and thread
- Scissors
- Single size 38 triangle felting needle

1) Add the facial features to your figure.

2) For the hair, use white merino wool to give the appearance of long straight hair. Pull off a 20 cm (8 in) length. Place over the figure's head and needle a parting. The merino wool will measure 10 cm (4 in) on each side of the parting. Gently needle the hair over the head.

3) The swimsuit for this figure is made from a pair of brightly coloured fishnet tights. I measured the foot of the tights against the figure and cut it to size. Don't worry if you cut it too small – it will enhance the busty look.

4) Using the template provided, cut out two holes for legs. Gently pull the swimsuit onto your figure.

5) Fold over the top raw edge and tuck it inside. Lightly needle the fishnet into place.

The Surfer

The surf's up dude.

You will need

- Needle-felted male figure, made following the instructions for Making a Felted Figure
- Light blue wool, for the irises
- Red wool, for the lips
- Brown wool, for the eyebrows and eyelashes
- White wool, for the eyes and teeth
- Pale yellow wool, for the hair and chest hair
- Orange wool, for the shorts
- Golden wool, for the shorts' band and trim
- Green wool, for the pattern on he shorts
- Single 38 and 40 triangle felting needles

1) Add the facial features to the figure. Use blue wool for the irises and brown wool for the eyebrows and eyelashes.

2) For the hair, place a piece of the pale yellow wool on the head and needle a parting to one side. Flop the longer length of hair over the face and form into a bouffant, floppy hairstyle. Needle gently into place using a size 40 needle.

3) This character has a toothy grin. For the mouth, roll a small piece of red wool between your fingers. Form into a half-moon shape and needle onto the face at a slight angle.

4) For the teeth, roll a wisp of white wool between your fingers and place in the middle of the mouth. Needle into place making sure the red lips show all around.

5) Needle a wisp of pale yellow wool over the chest as hair.

6) For the shorts, take a handful of orange wool and wrap it around the lower torso and half way down the thighs. Needle into place.

7) For the waistband, roll a piece of golden wool between your fingers into a sausage shape that will fit around the waist. Flatten it slightly on the pad before wrapping around the figure. Needle gently into place using small wisps of golden wool to cover the join.

8) For the turn-ups at the bottom of each leg of the shorts, roll a small piece of golden wool into a sausage shape that fits around each leg of the shorts. Needle into place.

9) For the pattern on the shorts, roll a small piece of green wool between your fingers to make a thin sausage. Needle into place as a wiggling stalk.

10) To add leaves to the stalk, take small pieces of green wool and needle onto the shorts in the shape of leaves. Place randomly up the green stalk.

The Lads

The Holiday Maker

Honestly, I'm not looking at page 3!

You will need

- Needle-felted male figure, made following the instructions for Making a Felted Figure

- Mottled brown wool, for hair, moustache, eyebrows, eyelashes and chest hair

- Red wool, for the swimming shorts and mouth

- Blue wool, for the eyes

- Black wool, for the pupils

- White wool, for the trim on the shorts, eyes and sailor's hat

- Use of a computer, printer and paper

- Scissors

- Glue

- 2 clothes pegs (clothes pins)

- Single size 38 triangle felting needle

1) Add the facial features to your figure. To make a moustache, use wisps of brown and needle between the lips and nose.

2) To make the hairy chest, needle wisps of brown wool onto the chest area.

3) To make the shorts, take a handful of red wool. Needle it around the figure from the waist to halfway down the thighs.

4) For the stripe on the shorts, roll a wisp of white wool between your fingers into a sausage shape. Needle it down the side of the shorts. Repeat on the other side.

5) To make the hat, take a handful of white wool and manipulate it into a circle. Needle it on the pad until you have a hat shape. Use the template provided as a guide to size. It needs to be very firm and at least 1 cm

(3/8 in) deep. Attach it to the head by needling until secure.

6) Using a computer, type out KISS ME QUICK on a black background. Print, then cut out so that it will fit around the hat. Glue in place ensuring the writing is at the front.

7) Use your computer to create a newspaper 5 x 7 cm (2 x 2¾ in). Print and cut out. Glue the paper into the figure's hands. Use clothes pegs to hold in place until the glue has dried.

THE REVELLER

The morning after the night before.

You will need

- Needle-felted male figure, made following the instructions for Making a Felted Figure
- White wool, for the eyes, socks, vest and sailor hat
- Brown wool, for the eyes, eyebrows, eyelashes, sandals and shorts
- Black wool, for the pupils
- Use of a computer, printer and paper
- Scissors
- Glue
- Single size 38 triangle felting needle

1) Add the facial features to your figure. Make the irises and beard dark brown.

2) To make the vest, take a handful of white wool. Wrap it around the upper torso and down as far as the waist. Shape into a vest and needle into place.

3) To make each sock, take a small handful of white wool and wrap it around the foot and ankle. Needle into place.

4) To make the shorts, take a handful of brown wool and wrap it around the lower torso down to the knees. Needle into place.

5) To make each sandal, take a small piece of brown wool. Place it over the top of the foot to form the strap, then needle into place.

6) To form the sole of the sandal, scrunch a small piece of brown wool in your fingers and place on the underside of the foot. Needle it into place. Be very careful not to stab your fingers.

7) Bend the arms and needle the hands to the sides of the body just below the waist so that he has his hands on his hips.

8) Needle a small piece of brown wool over each hand to give the impression that he has his hands in his pockets.

10) To make the hat, follow the instructions for The Holiday Maker

Anyone For Tennis?

The poster of the tennis player who forgot her pants was iconic in the 1970s.

You can make your own version.

You will need

- Needle-felted female figure, made following the instructions for Making a Felted Figure

- Brown wool, for the eyebrows, eyelashes and hair

- Red wool, for the lips and headband

- Blue wool, for the irises and trainers

- Black wool, for the pupils

- Light brown wool, for the soles of the trainers

- Cream wool, for the socks

- White wool, for the dress, eyes and trainers

- 4-felting needle holder fitted with triangle size 38 needles, plus 1 extra needle

- Tracing paper

- White card (card stock), for the tennis racket

- Glue

- Scissors

- Clothes peg (clothes pin)

- Small piece of net fabric, for the tennis racket

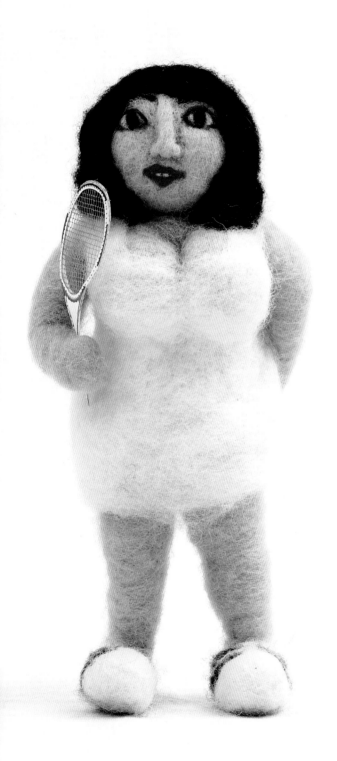

1) Add the facial features to the figure. Use brown wool for the hair.

2) To make each trainer, wrap a piece of white wool around the foot to form a shoe and needle into place.

3) To make each sock, roll a piece of cream wool between your fingers to make a sausage. Wrap around the ankle and needle the short sock into place.

4) For the sole of each trainer, needle a small piece of light brown wool across the underside of the trainer to make a sole. Take a thin wisp of the blue wool, roll it into a thin sausage with your fingers and place diagonally on the trainer just above the toes. Take another piece of blue wool and repeat the process, this time placing it a bit further up the shoe.

5) To make the dress, take a handful of white wool and wrap it around the upper torso to make a sleeveless top. Needle into place.

6) To make the skirt, take a handful of white wool and place it on the pad. Pull into a mini-skirt shape that will fit around the figure. Needle the wool using the 4-prong needle holder and work on the pad until you have a firm matted piece. Attach to the waist. Place the join over the cheek of the bottom you will expose.

7) Take the corresponding arm and bring it behind your tennis player, pushing the skirt up. Needle the hand in place on the bottom. Position the other arm so it is ready hold the tennis racket.

8) Tidy up the skirt at the back, needling creases in the skirt above the bottom.

9) To make the headband, roll a wisp of red wool between your fingers and attach over the hair. Needle the wool ends into the hair.

10) To make a tennis racket, trace 2 rackets from the template provided. Trace onto card and cut out. Be very careful when cutting out the middle section. Using the template provided, cut out the net. Spread glue on one card racket. Arrange the net over the centre to form the strings of the racket. Place the second racket on top of the first, sandwiching the net between the two. Leave to dry. Glue into the remaining hand, holding it in place with a clothes peg until dry.

The Royal Family
THE QUEEN

When the Queen of England comes to visit everyone's on their best behaviour.

You will need

- Needle-felted female figure, made following the instructions for Making a Felted Figure
- Grey wool, for the hair, eyebrows and eyelashes
- Red wool, for the lips
- White wool, for the eyes, gloves and shoes
- Black wool, for the pupils
- Pink wool, for the dress
- Single size 38 triangle felting needle
- 4-felting needle holder fitted with triangle size 38 needles
- Small pearl beads, for necklace
- Two small pearl, rhinestones for earrings

- A short length of fine chain
- A short piece of a jewelled braid
- Craft wire
- Crystal beads, for the tiara
- Glue
- Sewing needle and thread
- Scissors
- Pliers or wire cutters

1) Add the facial features to the figure. Add ears. Use grey wool for the eyelashes and eyebrows.

2) Using grey wool, form the hairstyle and needle it around the ears and the head.

3) To make the top of the dress, wrap a handful of pink wool around the upper torso. Make sure the neckline is low enough to have a visible necklace above. Add cap sleeves. Needle in place.

4) To form the skirt, take a handful of pink wool. Arrange it on the pad. Make sure the piece is wide enough to fit around the figure and long enough to make a maxi skirt. Using the 4-prong needle holder, needle the wool on the pad to a firm matted piece, turning it once. Wrap it around the lower torso, attaching to the waist before gently needling the seam of the skirt closed. Add wisps of wool to the join at the waist to give the appearance of a dress.

5) To make each shoe, wrap a small handful of white wool around the foot, shaping it into a shoe. Needle into place.

6) To make each long glove, wrap a small piece of white wool around the hand and arm up to the elbow. Needle into place.

7) To make earrings, dab the two pearl rhinestones with glue and stick to the ears.

8) To make the necklace, thread the pearl beads onto the thread. Position on the neck and tie the thread in a knot at the back of the head. Needle some grey hair over the knot.

9) To make the tiara, thread the craft wire with crystal beads. Form into a tiara shape using the template provided for the maid's cap. Push the tiara into the hair and gently needle wisps of grey wool around it to hold it in place.

10) To make the bag handle, cut a piece of chain using wire cutters.

11) Cut the bag shape from jewelled braid using the template provided.

12) Using the template, transfer the fold markings to the wrong side of the braid before spreading the inside of braid with glue. Place the ends of the chain across one inside fold to make a bag handle. Take a small piece of wool to bulk out the inside of the bag. Holding the chain in place, fold the bag up.

13) Bend one of the arms. Hang the chain over the bent arm and gently needle the arm to the body to hold the bag in place.

PRINCE PHILIP

Prince Philip always walks with his hands behind his back. Small details such as this add realistic character.

You will need

- Needle-felted male figure, made following the instructions for Making a Felted Figure

- Flesh-coloured wool, for the ears

- Blue wool, for the eyes

- Red wool, for the lips

- Grey wool, for the eyebrows, eyelashes and hair

- Black wool, for the jacket, trousers, tie, shoes and pupils

- White wool, for the shirt, handkerchief and socks

- Single size 38 triangle felting needle

- 4-felting needle holder fitted with triangle size 38 needles

1) Add the facial features to your figure. Use grey wool for the eyelashes and eyebrows.

2) Prince Philip has large ears so when making the ears use a larger amount of flesh-coloured wool and make a larger fold.

4) For the hair, needle a handful of grey wool around the ears and over the head. The hair is thinning at the front.

4) To make the shirt, arrange a piece of white wool on the front of the figure and needle from the chin to the waist.

5) To make each shoe, wrap black wool around each foot to make a shoe shape and needle it into place.

6) To make each sock, roll a small piece of white wool into a short fat sausage and wrap around the ankle. Needle into place, ensuring it is attached firmly to the top of the shoe.

7) To make the trousers, take a handful of black wool and cover the lower torso and bottom, wrapping around the legs. Needle into place.

8) For the jacket, arrange a handful of black wool on the pad and pull it into the shape of a jacket, using the template provided. Using the 4-prong needle holder, needle the wool until matted and firm, turning it once. Wrap around the figure and attach at the shoulders and front. Wrap more wool around the arms and needle the sleeves into place. Add more wisps of wool until satisfied.

9) To make the collar, roll a small piece of black wool between your fingers into a sausage. Needle the jacket collar onto the jacket.

10) To make the shirt collar, roll a small piece of white wool between your fingers until it is a sausage shape and fits around the neck. Arrange on the pad and needle flat. Wrap the white collar around the neck and needle in place.

11) To make the tie, roll a small piece of black wool into a ball. Take a similar size piece of black wool and roll into a sausage. Place the ball at the neck between the collar ends. Arrange the tie front down the centre of the chest. Needle both into place.

12) To form a pocket, place a small piece of black wool on the left side of the jacket at the breast point. Needle into shape, leaving the top open.

13) Take a smaller piece of white wool and push into the breast pocket, leaving a little bit showing. Gently needle to resemble a handkerchief.

PRINCE WILLIAM, DUKE OF CAMBRIDGE

The heir to the throne is one happy chappy.

You will need

- Needle-felted male figure, made following the instructions for Making a Felted Figure

- White wool, for the eyes, teeth and shirt

- Brown wool, for the trousers, hair, eyebrows and eyelashes

- Black wool, for the shoes and pupils

- Blue wool, for the eyes

- Red wool, for the lips

- Single size 38 triangle felting needle

1) Add the facial features to your figure. For the mouth, roll a small piece of red wool lightly between your fingers into a half-moon shape. Position on the face and needle in place.

2) For the teeth, take a smaller piece of white wool and shape as before. Centre on the mouth and needle gently, making sure that the red of the lips shows all around the teeth.

3) Use blue wool to form the irises.

4) Make the ears large.

5) Make the hairline recede.

6) For the shirt, take some white wool and wrap around the upper torso. Leave the centre front open. Needle into place. For the sleeves, wrap white wool around his arms, and needle into place.

7) To form the collar, roll a piece of white wool into a long sausage that will go all the way around the neck. Arrange on the pad and needle flat. Attach the collar to the neck of the shirt. Needle into place leaving some of the neck and chest showing.

8) To make the trousers, wrap pieces of brown wool around the lower torso and legs. Needle into place.

9) To make each shoe, wrap a piece of black wool around each foot. Needle into place.

THE DUCHESS OF CAMBRIDGE

Very stylish.

You will need

- Needle-felted female figure, made following the instructions for Making a Felted Figure
- Light blue wool, for the dress and irises
- White wool, for the shoes, eyes, teeth and polka dots
- Brown wool, for the eyebrows and eyelashes
- Brown alpaca wool, for the hair
- Black wool, for the pupils
- Red wool, for the lips
- Single size 38 triangle felting needle
- 4-felting needle holder fitted with triangle size 38 needles

1) Add facial features to your figure. For the mouth, roll a small piece of red wool lightly between your fingers into a half-moon shape. Position on the face and needle in place.

2) For the teeth, take a smaller piece of white wool and shape as before. Centre on the mouth and needle gently, making sure that the red of the lips shows all around the teeth.

3) For the hair, pull off a 20 cm (8 in) in length of the rope-like alpaca wool. Centre it over the head and needle a centre parting. Gently needle the hair over the head.

4) Wrap some of the light blue wool around the torso in the style of a dress top. Needle into place. Wrap smaller pieces of light blue wool around the top of each arm to make short sleeves. Needle into place.

5) For the skirt, take a larger piece of light blue wool. Make sure it is wide enough to fit around the figure and long enough to reach the knees. Place on the pad and needle using the 4-prong needle holder until flat and firm, turning once. Wrap around the figure placing the joining at the back. Needle firmly around the waist and gently down the back seam. Add wisps of light blue wool to hide the seam. Needle gently.

6) Roll small pinches of white wool in your fingers for the polka dots. Make 18. Take a ball and needle gently onto the dress. Repeat to give the impression of polka dots.

7) To make each court shoe, wrap a piece of white wool around each foot. Needle into place.

BABY PRINCE GEORGE

This little bundle will wear a crown one day.

You will need

- Flesh-coloured wool, for the head
- White wool, for the shawl
- Brown wool, for the hair
- Red wool, for the mouth
- Single size 38 triangle felting needle
- 4-felting needle holder fitted with triangle size 38 needles

1) Using flesh-coloured wool, make a 3 cm (1¼ in) diameter ball for the head, following the instructions for Making the Head.

2) To make the nose, roll a wisp of flesh-coloured wool between your fingers to make a ball. Needle gently onto the face.

3) To make sleeping eyes, roll two wisps of brown wool between your fingers and shape into crescents. Needle gently on baby's face.

4) For the mouth, take a wisp of red wool. Roll into a tiny ball and needle gently into an 'O' shape.

5) For the hair, take some brown wool and cover the rest of the head thinly.

6) To make the shawl, place a handful of white wool on the pad and using the 4-needle holder, needle flat into a rectangle, turning once. Swaddle around the head. Stuff the body area with leftover wool and make a rotund body. Needle the shawl around baby. Needle in Kate's arms.

French Maid

Oo saucy! A perfect cheeky gift.

You will need

- Needle-felted female figure, made following the instructions for Making a Felted Figure

- White wool, for the eyes and dress trim

- Red wool, for the lips

- Blue wool, for the irises

- Brown wool, for the eyebrows and eyelashes

- Black wool, for the dress, stocking trim, suspenders, hair, shoes and pupils

- Black fishnet tights

- Broderie Anglaise braid, 6 cm (2½ in) wide

- Narrow white lace, for the apron and cap trim

- Thin white ribbon

- Sewing needle and thread

- Scissors

- Single size 40 triangle felting needle

- 4-felting needle holder fitted with size 38 triangle felting needles

1) Add facial features to your figure. Use black wool for the hair.

2) To make the stockings, using the template provided, cut 2 from fishnet stocking. Sew up the seams, turn inside out and gently roll up the legs of the figure.

3) Wrap a wisp of black wool around the stocking tops and needle into place.

4) For the suspenders, take four wisps of black wool and arrange each vertically from the stocking tops to the waist. Needle gently into place, using the 40-gauge needle.

5) For each shoe, wrap a small piece of black wool around each foot and needle in place. For the sole, roll a small piece of black wool into a ball and add to the heel. Continue to add small wisps of black wool until your shoe has a small lump at the heel for kitten heels.

6) Take a handful of black wool and place on the pad. Shape into a mini-skirt, measuring the size against the figure. Remember her stocking tops should show so don't make it too long. Using the 4-prong needle holder, needle the wool until flat and matted on the pad, then attach to the figure's waist. Add wisps of wool to hide the seam.

7) Finish the maid's dress by needling black wool to the figure's top. As the maid is cheeky she will show some of her bust.

8) Wrap some more black wool around the arms to make short sleeves.

9) For the collar, roll some white wool between your fingers. Needle around the

neck of the dress.

10) To make cuffs for the sleeves, roll a smaller piece of white wool between your fingers then wrap around the sleeves. Needle into place.

11) From broderie Anglaise braid, cut an apron using the template provided. Stitch the thin lace around the curved edge of the apron to form a frill, pleating the lace as you stitch. Now sew the straight edge of the apron on to the waistband (the white ribbon). Make sure you place your apron in the centre so that you have equal lengths of ribbon on each side. Tie the apron around the waist of the figure trimming off any excess.

12) Make the cap from a piece of the thin lace using the template as a guide. Stitch to the head, then needle more black wool onto the figure's head behind the cap to make the cap stand up..

The Golfer

Make this mascot for a golfing fanatic's desk.

You will need

- Needle-felted male figure, made following the instructions for Making a Felted Figure

- Light brown wool, for the cap, plus four trousers, brogues and bow tie

- Dark brown wool, for the soles, hair, eyebrows and eyelashes

- White wool, for the top, brogues, socks and eyes

- Golden yellow wool, for the pullover

- Green wool, for the socks

- Red wool, for the lips

- Black wool, for the pupils and shoe laces

- Single size 38 triangle felting needle

- Wooden skewer or a length of thin round wood, for the golf club

- A small piece of balsa wood, for the golf club

- Silver acrylic paint, for the golf club

- Black acrylic paint, for the golf club

- Craft knife, for the golf club

- Craft glue

1) Add the facial features to your figure. For the mouth, roll a wisp of red wool between your fingers. Fold one side inward so that the shape is thicker on one side. Needle to the face in a slight upward curve.

2) Use blue wool for the irises.

3) For the shirt, wrap some white wool around the upper torso. Needle into place. For the sleeves, wrap small pieces around the arms down to the hands. Needle into place.

4) To make the plus-four trousers, wrap light brown wool around the lower torso and upper legs. Needle into place. These are wide-leg trousers that finish below the knee.

5) For each sock, cover the lower leg and the top of the foot in white wool. Needle into place.

6) For the sole of each shoe, needle a dark brown wool sole onto the underside of each foot.

7) For each shoe upper, make a strap over each foot using light brown wool. Needle into place.

8) For the shoe laces, roll a small piece of black wool into a very thin sausage. Arrange on the shoe in a criss-cross pattern to resemble laces. Needle gently into place. Repeat on the other shoe.

9) For the pattern on the socks, take 4 small pieces of light brown wool and needle into diamond shapes. Repeat to make another 4 green diamonds. Needle these to the socks.

10) For the pullover, arrange a handful of the golden yellow wool in place, using the template provided as a guide and needle onto the body.

11) For the bow tie, needle a small piece of light brown wool into a rectangle. Wrap another small piece of light brown wool around the middle of the rectangle, tightening it to make a bow. Needle onto the figure at the throat.

12) Using the template provided for the cap, make a firm light brown matted circle using the pad. Keep the sides low and build up the middle into a domed shape. Attach firmly to the head.

13) For the peak of the cap, shape a smaller piece of light brown wool into a crescent using the template as a guide. Needle on the pad until it is a firm, thin flat shape, then attach to the front of the cap and head.

14) To make the golf club, measure the wooden stick against the figure and trim at lower chest height.

15) Shape the balsa wood into a club and glue to the base of the stick. Leave to dry. Paint the golf club silver and black.

Ballerina

Make your own sugar plum fairy.

You will need

- Needle-felted female figure, made following the instructions for Making a Felted Figure

- White wool, for the leotard, ballet pumps and eyes

- Red wool, for the lips

- Blue wool, for the irises

- Black wool, for the pupils

- Light brown wool, for the eyelashes and eyebrows

- Rust-coloured wool, for the hair

- 1 m (1 yd) of thin white ribbon, for the ballet pumps and hairstyle holder

- Thin white feather boa, for the skirt and hair

- White net, for the tutu

- Sewing needle and white thread

- Felting needles

- Single size 40 triangle felting needle

1) Add facial features to the figure. Use light brown wool for the eyebrows and eyelashes.

2) For the hair, arrange a handful of rust wool so that it begins at the neck, with the bulk of the wool down the figure's back, leaving the head bald. Needle firmly around the hairline at the back of the neck from ear to ear. Then lift the rust wool up and over the head. Needle the hair gently onto the top of the head. Form a bun and needle firmly in place. Wrap a piece of white ribbon around the bun and stitch into place. Pull a few feathers from the boa and needle these around the bun on top of the ribbon using the size 40 felting needle.

3) To make the leotard, use white wool and follow the instructions for making the swimsuit on page 38.

4) To make each ballet pump, take a small piece of white wool and flatten it. Wrap it around the foot. Needle into place. Repeat with the other foot.

5) Cut the ribbon into four equal lengths. Take the end of one length and sew it to the left side of a foot, close to the toes on the edge of the pump. Repeat on the other side of the shoe. Hide the stitched part of the ribbon with wisps of wool, if you like. Criss-cross the ribbons around and up the legs to the knees, then tie the ends of the laces together to make a knot at the back of the knees. Do not to pull the ribbon laces too tight or they will dig into the legs. Make a few stitches where the ribbons cross to hold them in place. Repeat with the other leg.

6) To make the tutu, cut 2 long lengths of net and run a gathering thread through them. Pull up tightly and wrap around the waist. Stitch to the figure at the waist to secure.

7) Wrap the feather boa around the waist on top of the net tutu. Stitch firmly in place. Needle gently into place.

Outback Explorer

This handsome chap has befriended a koala while roaming the outback.

You will need

- Needle-felted male figure, made following the instructions for Making a Felted Figure
- Light grey wool, for the shirt, belt-buckle and socks
- Mid-brown wool, for the shorts, eyebrows and eyes
- Dark brown wool, for the hat, shoes and buttons
- Dark grey wool, for the hair
- White wool, for the eyes and teeth
- Red wool, for the mouth
- Single size 38 triangle felting needle

1) Add the facial features to your figure. Add ears and a nose. Make the hair dark grey.

2) For the toothy grin, roll a small piece of red wool between your fingers. Make a half-moon shape and needle this onto the face at a slight angle for the mouth.

3) Roll a wisp of white wool between your fingers and place in the middle of the mouth to represent the teeth. Needle into place, making sure the red lips show all around. Keep pushing the needle into the centre of the front of the teeth until there is a gap.

4) To make the eyes, use mid-brown wool for irises, eyebrows and eyelashes.

5) To make the shorts, needle a handful of mid-brown wool around the lower torso and halfway down the thighs. To make the turn-up at the bottom of the legs, roll a small amount of mid-brown wool into a sausage shape. Needle in place around the knee. Repeat on the other leg.

6) To make the shirt, needle some grey wool around the upper torso, leaving a V at the neckline. Wrap small pieces of grey wool around the top of the arms. Needle into place to make a short-sleeved shirt. Take a small piece of grey wool for the collar and roll between your fingers. Measure around the neck until it fits. Needle flat on your pad then attach to the shirt.

7) To make the buttonhole facing, roll a small piece of grey wool between your fingers and position it down one side of the neck opening. Needle gently into place. Attach a second piece to the other side of the open neck area.

8) To make the shirt pockets, take a small piece of grey wool and needle into a square shape, curved at one end. Make 2. Needle in place on the shirt.

9) For the shirt buttons, roll tiny pieces of dark brown wool into balls. Gently needle onto the buttonhole facing. Add a button to each pocket.

10) To make the belt, roll a piece of mid-brown wool between your fingers to a sausage shape that fits around the waist. Flatten it slightly on the pad before

wrapping around the figure. Needle gently into place.

11) For the belt buckle, roll a small piece of grey wool into a ball. Needle over the belt at the centre front.

12) Bend the arms, placing the hands on the hips. Take a small piece of mid-brown wool and needle over the hands to give the impression that the hands are in the pockets.

13) For each sock, roll a small piece of grey wool into a sausage. Place around the ankle and needle into place.

14) For each boot, take a piece of brown wool and flatten it. Fold it around the foot. Needle into place. Repeat on the other foot.

15) For the hat brim, shape a piece of brown wool into a circle, matching it against the template provided and needle until firm.

16) For the crown, fold a clump of brown wool into a smaller circle using the template as a guide. Needle firmly; the depth of this piece is 2 cm (¾ in). Needle the brim and crown together before needling the hat onto the head at a jaunty angle. One side of the brim can be fixed to the crown, if you like.

The Medics

NURSE

And cough.

You will need

- Needle-felted female figure, made following the instructions for Making a Felted Figure
- Dull gold wool, for the hair
- Light brown wool, for the eyebrows and eyelashes
- Pair of black fishnet tights, for the tights
- Light blue wool, for the dress and irises
- Black wool, for the shoes, cape and pupils
- White wool, for the cap, apron and eyes
- Red wool, for the lips and cross bands
- Sewing needle and black cotton thread
- Felting needles
- Single size 38 triangle felting needle
- 4-prong needle holder fitted with triangle size 38 needles

1) Add the facial features to the figure. Make the shoulder length hair using dull-gold wool.

2) Take the fishnet tights and measure one leg against your figure or template provided. Cut off at the figure's waist. Cut up the middle from the foot to about three quarters of the way up (following the diagram). Stitch up the legs using a sewing needle and black cotton. Turn inside out, making your figure a small pair of tights. Gently pull these up the figure's legs and lower body. Needle the top around your figure's waist to hold them in place.

3) For each shoe, flatten a piece of black wool in your fingers. Fold it around the foot. Needle into place over the fishnet to make a sturdy shoe.

4) To make the skirt, take a piece of light blue wool and measure it to the figure, making sure it is long enough to cover the knees and fits all the way around the figure. Place the wool on the pad and needle until firm. Attach around the waist, needling gently with wisps of wool to hide the join.

5) To make the top, take a piece of light blue wool large enough to cover the upper torso and needle into place, covering the chest.

6) To make short sleeves, wrap the upper arms in light blue wool and needle in place.

7) For the sleeve cuff, wrap a small piece of white wool around each arm and needle into place.

8) To make a collar, roll a piece of white wool between your fingers long enough to

fit around the neck. Place on the pad and needle flat. Attach to the neck.

9) For the apron skirt, pull a piece of white wool into a square shape, making sure you measure it against the figure. Needle on the pad until firm. Attach at the waist. Repeat to make the apron bib. Needle gently onto the chest and firmly at the waist.

10) To make apron strings, roll a small piece of white wool between your fingers to make a strip. Flatten by needling gently on the pad before arranging over one shoulder and attaching from the top of the pinafore to the waist. Needle in place. Make another for the strap over the other shoulder.

11) To make the hat, take a small piece of white wool and using the template provided, create the shape. Flatten the piece on the pad and needle it so that it is firm. Needle the cap onto the head and into the hair. Add wisps of dull gold wool behind the cap to make sure it stands up.

12) To make the cloak, take a large piece of black wool and tease it into shape using the template provided. Transfer to the pad and needle until firm, turning it once. Use the set of four needles for this process. Attach to the back of the neck starting just above the collar, and ensuring the rounded corners are wider at the base of the cloak. Needle firmly into place with a single needle.

13) Take the red wool and roll into a thin sausage shape. Needle it at the top left of the neck at the cloak and bring it across the bust needling it to the figure's right side, half way down the bust. Repeat to make another strap to criss cross the first one. Needle the cloak edges in place over the shoulders.

DOCTOR

Is there a doctor in the house?

You will need

- Needle-felted female figure, made following the instructions for Making a Felted Figure

- Light blue wool, for the overalls

- White wool, for the eyes and shoes

- Mid-brown wool, for the irises

- Black wool, for the hair, eyebrows, eyelashes and pupils

- Red wool, for the lips

- Single size 38 triangle felting needle

- Toy stethoscope

1) Add the facial features to your figure. Add white eyes and dark brown irises. Add black wool eyebrows and eyelashes. Add black wool shoulder length hair. Using red wool, form lips.

2) For the trousers, wrap a handful of light blue wool around the lower torso and all the way down the legs. Add more wool as needed. Needle into place.

3) For the top, wrap a clump of light blue wool around the torso top, leaving a V at the neckline. Needle into place. Take small pieces of light blue wool and wrap around the arms. Needle into place to give long sleeves.

4) To make each shoe, flatten a piece of white wool, fold it around the foot and needle into place.

5) Place the toy stethoscope around the neck. Doctors place the end of their stethoscope in a pocket. Take a small piece of light blue wool and needle over the end of the stethoscope to give the impression of a pocket.

THE PATIENT

Wearing nothing but his birthday suit, this patient is easy to model.

You will need

- Needle-felted male figure, made following the instructions for Making a Felted Figure
- White wool, for the eyes and teeth
- Black wool, for the eyes
- Red wool, for the mouth
- Brown wool, for the eyebrows, eyelashes and hair

1) Add facial features to your figure. For the mouth, take a small piece of red wool and roll it into a ball, needle on to the face to make a round, open mouth.

2) For the teeth, take a smaller piece of white wool. Roll into a ball and needle into the centre of the mouth, giving your figure a surprised look.

3) Give the male figure short sideburns using brown wool. This will successfully cover the ear join.

4) Needle his hands into place.

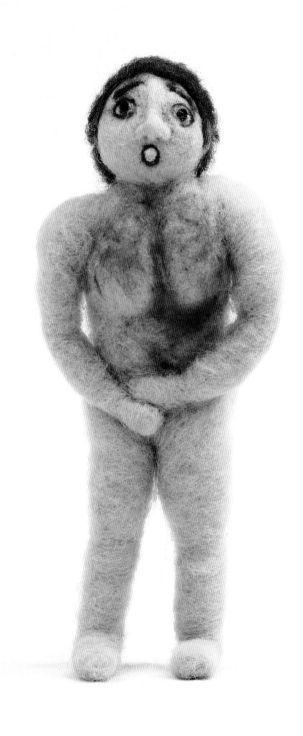

Rugby Players

Come on you Wallabies! Come on you All Blacks!

THE ALL-BLACK

You will need

- Needle-felted male figure, made following the instructions for Making a Felted Figure
- Black wool, for the socks, shoes, shorts, top, hair, sweatbands, inside mouth, eyebrows and eyelashes
- White wool, for the trimmings, teeth and eyes
- Mid-brown wool, for the irises
- Red wool, for the lips
- Single size 38 triangle felting needle

1) Add the facial features to the figure. This character has a snarl. Roll a small piece of red wool between your fingers and form it into an oval shape for the mouth. Needle it onto the face.

2) For the teeth, roll a wisp of white wool between your fingers. Needle upper and lower teeth in place making sure that the red lips shows all around. To fill the gap between the teeth, take a wisp of black wool and needle it into the gap. Keep pushing the needle into the centre of the front of the teeth until you have made a gap between two front teeth. Repeat to form eight teeth.

3) Use mid-brown wool for the irises.

4) Use black wool for the eyelashes, hair and eyebrows. Place the front of the eyebrow close to the side of the nose and the corner of the eye. Angle each upward to create a menacing look.

5) To make the shorts, take a handful of black wool and needle it around the lower torso and halfway down the thighs.

6) To make the top, needle some more black wool around the upper torso. Wrap small pieces of black wool around the top of the arms to create short sleeves. Needle into place.

7) To make a collar, roll a small piece of white wool between your fingers to fit around the neck. Needle flat on the pad then attach to the neck of the shirt.

8) To form the shirt opening below the collar, roll a small piece of white wool between your fingers. Position on the front

of the shirt and needle gently into place.

9) Take another small piece of white wool and needle into a small triangle. Needle in place on the left breast. Take a small wisp of white wool and needle into a curled feather shape on the right breast.

10) To make each sock, wrap a small piece of black wool around each lower leg up to the knee. Needle into place.

11) To make each boot, flatten a pieces of black wool into a rectangle 10 x 5 cm (4 x 2 in) with your fingers. Fold around the foot, bringing the longer sections up around the ankle. Needle into place.

12) For each sweatband, wrap a piece of black wool around each wrist and needle into place.

13) For the sweatband decoration, take a small wisp of white wool and roll between your fingers to a thin sausage. Place in the middle of the black sweatband and needle into place. Repeat on the other sweatband, and at the top of each sock.

THE WALLABY

Scrum down with this handsome fella.

You will need

- Needle-felted male figure, made following the instructions for Making a Felted Figure

- Yellow wool, for the top, sock trim and trainers

- Green wool, for the shorts, collar, top trim and socks

- Brown wool, for the hair, moustache, eyebrows, eyelashes and irises

- White wool, for the eye, teeth and rugby ball

- Red wool, for the mouth

- Black wool, for the pupils and trainer trim

- Single size 38 triangle felting needle

- Light blue wool, for the ruby ball trim

1) Add the facial features to the figure. For the moustache, roll a small piece of brown wool between your fingers. Needle onto the face just above the mouth.

2) Use brown wool for irises, eyelashes, hair and eyebrows.

3) For the shorts, wrap a handful of green wool around the lower torso and halfway down the thighs. Needle in place.

4) For the top, wrap yellow wool around the upper torso, leaving a V at the neck. Take small pieces of yellow wool and wrap around the top of the arms for sleeves. Needle into place.

5) Roll a small piece of green wool between your fingers for the collar. Needle flat on the pad, then attach to the collar of the shirt.

6) For the collar opening, roll a small piece of green wool between your fingers. Place on the top centre front of the shirt. Needle gently into place.

7) For the decorative triangle on the left breast, form a small piece of green wool into shape. Needle into place.

8) Take a small wisp of brown wool and needle into a wallaby shape on the right breast.

9) To make each sock, wrap a small piece of green wool around the lower leg up to the knee and needle into place.

10) For each boot, take a piece of yellow wool and flatten it. Fold around the foot. Needle into place.

11) Roll a wisp of black wool between your fingers and arrange as a strip on the trainer. Make 2 on each side of each shoe.

13) Roll a wisp of yellow wool between your fingers to a thin sausage shape. Place on the top of a sock and needle into place. Repeat on the other sock.

14) To make the rugby ball, roll some white wool into an oval ball. Needle until firm.

15) Roll a wisp of light blue wool between your fingers and arrange along the length of the ball to give a striped effect. Needle into place.

16) Needle the ball onto the rugby player's hands.

The American Football Team

Have great fun making contenders for the superbowl.

THE FOOTBALLER

You will need

- Needle-felted male figure, made following the instructions for Making a Felted Figure
- White wool, for the top, shorts, shoes and eyes
- Blue wool, for the socks and trims
- Black wool, for the hair, eyelashes, eyebrows, pupils and war paint
- Red wool, for the mouth
- Single size 38 triangle felting needle
- Brown wool, for the football
- Orange wool, for the football

1) Add the facial features to the figure. To make the turned-down mouth, roll a small piece of red wool between your fingers. Fold one end over so that it is thicker at that end. Place on the face in a downward crescent and needle onto the face.

2) Use brown wool for the irises, and black wool for the eyelashes, hair, eyebrows and two strips of war paint under the eyes.

3) For the shorts, wrap a handful of white wool around the lower torso and halfway down the thighs to the knees. Needle into place.

4) For the top, wrap a handful of white wool around the upper torso and needle into place to make a vest. Wrap small pieces of white wool around the top of the arms. Needle into place to form short sleeves.

Now begin to build his shoulders up and out. Needle into place.

5) To make the collar, roll a small piece of blue wool between your fingers. Measure to fit around the neck. Needle into place.

6) To form the stripes at the base of each sleeve, roll a small piece of blue wool between your fingers. Wrap around the sleeves. Needle into place.

7) Roll a wisp of blue wool into a thin sausage. Place on the left side of the chest. Form into the shape of a five and needle gently into place. Repeat on the right side to make the number 55. Now do the same on each shoulder making smaller 55s.

8) To make each sock, wrap a piece of blue wool around the lower leg up to the bottom

edge of the shorts. Needle into place.

9) For each training shoe flatten a piece of white wool into a rectangle approximately 10 x 5 cm (4 x 2 in). Wrap around one foot, placing the toes and heel in the shorter section and folding the longer sections up around the ankle. Fold all the wool around the foot. Needle into place.

10) For the football, roll some brown wool into an oval ball. Needle until firm.

11) Take 2 wisps of orange wool, roll between your fingers and arrange as stripes around each end of the ball. Needle into place.

12) Needle the ball into the American footballer's hand.

THE CHEERLEADER

These girls have a lot of charm. You can easily make them in your team's colours.

You will need

- Needle-felted female figure, made following the instructions for Making a Felted Figure

- Blue wool, for the bra and pants, irises, and sandals

- Red wool, for the lips, bra and pants,

- White wool, for the eyes and costume trim

- Black wool, for the eyelashes, eyebrows and pupils

- Choice of wool shade for the hair

- Single size 38 triangle felting needle

- Two pom-poms

1) Add the facial features to the figure. Use blue wool for the irises and black wool for the eyes and eyebrows.

2) Add the hair using any wool shade of your choice.

3) To make the pants, take a small handful of blue wool and needle over the lower torso.

4) For the bra, roll some blue wool into a thin long rectangle. Wrap it around the bust and back forming a bikini top. Needle into place starting under the bust. This wool should cover most of the bust but not be too thick around the back.

5) Pull a small piece of red wool into a pizza slice shape (3 x 3 x 2 cm/1¼ x 1¼ x ¾ in). Place over the top of the bust and up to the top of the shoulder with the smaller side of the triangle up toward the shoulder. Needle into place. Repeat on the other side. Cover the figure's back from the top of the bra to the neck with red wool and needle into place.

6) Roll a piece of red wool between your fingers into a long fat sausage. Arrange around the top of the pants. Needle firmly into place making sure it doesn't cover the figure's midriff.

7) Roll a small piece of white wool between your fingers into a long thin sausage. Arrange on the pants where the red and blue meet and needle into place. Make another and place on the top edge of the pants.

8) Repeat to add a white stripe on the bra between the red and blue wools and needle into place. Take another small piece of white

wool and arrange along the top edge of the bra cups and needle into place.

9) Wrap a small piece of blue wool over the foot and needle into place to make a sandal strap. Shape a piece of blue wool into a sole, needling on the pad before needling onto the underside of the foot to make an open-toed sandal. Repeat with the other foot.

The Motorcycle Cop

I didn't realise I was going that fast officer!

You will need

- Needle-felted male figure, made following the instructions for Making a Felted Figure

- Brown wool, for the irises

- Black wool, for the beard, hair, eyelashes, eyebrows, pupils, motorcycle jacket and boots

- White wool, for the trousers, neck tie, eyes and glass visor

- Light blue wool, for the shirt

- Small piece of leather, for the belt

- Glue

- Silver belt buckle

- Police badge

- Single sizes 38 and 40 triangle felting needles

- 4-prong needle holder fitted with triangle size 38 needles

1) Add the facial features to the figure. He has a black beard, eyebrows and eyelashes and brown eyes.

2) For the shirt, take a clump of light blue wool. Needle over the front of the figure from the neck to the waist. Leave a V-neck.

3) For the trousers, take a handful of white wool and wrap over the lower torso and legs and needle into place.

4) To make each motorcycle boot, wrap a piece of black wool around the foot and lower calf. Add more wool, if needed, and then needle firmly. Add a small piece of wool to the underside of the boot to make a sole. Needle into place.

5) For the biker's jacket, take a handful of black wool and using the template provided, pull into shape. Place on the pad and using the 4-prong needle holder, needle until the piece is firm and matted, turning once. Attach to the figure at the shoulders and front, adding wisps of black wool to hide the seams. As biker jackets are slightly bloused, gently needle the jacket to the upper torso using a size 40 single felting needle. Leave the front of the jacket open to reveal some blue shirt.

6) For the sleeves, wrap a piece of black wool around the arms down to the hands, needle gently until you are satisfied with the look of the jacket.

7) For the collar, roll a small piece of blue wool between your fingers to fit around the neck. Needle flat on the pad, then attach the collar to the shirt, arranging it over the jacket.

8) For the scarf, pull a piece of white wool into a long thin rectangle and needle on the pad. When it is long enough, wrap around the neck, above the blue collar, and form a tie, needling the ends onto the figure.

9) Using the sailor's hat template provided as a guide to size, make the hat. Take a clump of black wool, fold up the sides, and build the domed shape of a motorcycle helmet. Needle until you have a firm matted dome. Needle firmly onto the head.

10) Take a small piece of white wool. Pull into a rectangle and needle onto the helmet as a visor.

11) Cut the leather into a thin belt to hang just below the waist. Cut out two holsters using the template provided. Make two slits in the top of each holster. Thread the belt

through the slits and then wrap the belt around the figure. Using glue, stick the ends together and then glue a buckle over the join. Position the holsters on each side of he body.

12) Print a small picture of a police badge and cut it out. Glue in place on the left-hand side of the chest

MR and MRS

A perfect gift for newly weds.

THE BRIDE

You will need

- Needle-felted female figure, made following the instructions for Making a Felted Figure
- White wool, for the eyes, dress, shoes and teeth
- Black wool, for the eyes
- Brown wool, for the eyelashes and eyebrows
- Blue wool, for the irises
- Red merino wool, for the hair
- Red wool, for the mouth
- 60 cm (2 ft) net, for the dress
- Lace edging, for the dress
- White paper roses (available from craft shops), for the headdresss
- Red paper roses (available from craft shops), for the bouquet
- Sewing needle and white cotton thread
- Felting needles
- Single size 38 triangle felting needle
- 4-prong needle holder fitted with triangle size 38 needles

1) Add the facial features to the figure. Use brown wool for eyelashes and eyebrows. Use blue wool for the irises.

2) For the mouth, roll a small piece of red wool lightly between your fingers. Arrange on the face so it is curving upward and needle firmly into a half moon shape.

3) For the teeth, roll a smaller piece of white wool into a half-moon shape as before. Place in the middle of the mouth and needle gently, making sure that the red lips show all around the teeth. Needle firmly in the centre of the mouth to give the appearance of a gap between the teeth.

4) I used merino wool to fashion the hairstyle. As merino wool is combed and comes in long soft ropes it is easy to needle the wool into a wavy style. Pull 20 cm

(8 in) of wool from the rope. Centre over the bride's head and needle a parting down the centre of the head.

5) Working on one section of the head at a time, hold the hair in waves and gently needle in place to secure the hair to the head. Tuck the loose ends underneath the shoulders and needle into place. Continue around the head.

6) To make the top of the dress, wrap a handful of white wool around the upper torso, forming scallops over the bust to make a strapless gown.

7) For the skirt, pull a handful of white wool into a rectangle and place on the pad. Measure against the figure to make sure it is wide enough to go all the way around and that you have enough to make a maxi skirt.

Needle until firmly matted. Wrap around the lower half of the figure, attaching to the waist before gently needling the edges of the skirt closed.

8) For each shoe, wrap a small handful of white wool all around the foot, shaping into a sandal and needling into place.

9) Cut 4 lengths of net each 13 cm (5 in) wide for the dress. With a sewing needle and white thread, run large gathering stiches along one long side of each of the pieces. Make sure the thread it secure at the beginning so you don't end up pulling it out.

10) Pull the gathering thread so that the net pulls into ruffles. The skirt needs to be very full, so the more ruffles the better. Wrap each piece around the waist, one on top of the other, and stitch into place.

11) Stitch the lace edging over the waist edges to tidy the appearance between the skirt and the top.

12) Wrap the stalks of the white roses around each other to make a circlet that fits the bride's head. Take a rectangle of tulle net and stitch it three quarters of the way around the circlet to make a veil. Fix to the hair with small stitches and arrange the veil around the bride.

13) Position the hands together. Take the bunch of red roses and sew into the clasped hands.

THE GROOM

This dashing gentleman is a delight to make.

You will need

- Needle-felted male figure, made following the instruction for Making a Felted Figure

- Black wool for the suit, shoes, pupils, cravat, button and hat band

- White wool, for the shirt, socks and eyes

- Brown wool, for the hair, irises, eyelashes, beard and moustache

- Red wool, for the lips

- Tiny white paper rose (available from craft shops)

- Single size 38 triangle felting needle

- 4-prong needle holder fitted with triangle size 38 needles

1) Add the facial features to the figure. Use brown wool for the eyelashes, eyebrows, beard, moustache and hair.

2) For the shirt, arrange a small handful of white wool on the front torso of the figure and needle from chin to waist.

3) To make the collar, roll a small piece of white wool between your fingers into a sausage shape that fits around the neck. Place on the pad and needle flat. Needle the collar into place around the neck.

4) To make the cravat, roll a small piece of black wool between your fingers into a short sausage. Needle flat on the pad. Fold in half and arrange the fold at the front centre neck between the collar ends. Needle the cravat gently.

5) Roll a wisp of black wool into a ball between your fingers. Needle this into the centre of the chest, below the cravat, to make a shirt button.

6) To make each shoe, wrap a small amount of black wool around the foot. Needle into place.

7) To make each sock, roll a small piece of white wool between your fingers into a short sausage shape. Wrap around the ankle and needle into place. Make sure each is attached firmly to the top of the shoe.

8) For the trousers, take small handfuls of black wool and cover the lower torso, bottom, and legs. Needle into place.

9) To make the jacket, pull a handful of black wool into a jacket shape, using the template provided. Arrange on the pad and needle the wool until it is matted and firm, turning once. The 4-prong needle holder makes this easier and quicker.

10) Wrap the jacket around the figure and attach at the shoulders and front. For sleeves, wrap a piece of wool around one arm and needle into place. Add more wisps of wool as needed. Repeat on the other arm.

11) Roll a small piece of white wool between your fingers into a short sausage. Wrap around a wrist and needle into place to create a cuff. Repeat on the other side.

12) Roll a piece of black wool between your fingers into a long sausage. Measure against the neckline of the jacket until it is long enough to make a collar. Needle the collar gently onto the jacket.

13) To make gloves, wrap a small piece of grey wool around the figure's hands and needle into place.

14) For the hat, using the template provided for the top hat brim, take a piece of grey wool and fold the corners inward to create a circle to match the template shape. Place on the pad and needle until flat, firm and matted. Roll a handful of grey wool into a fat sausage 5 cm (2 in) long and the diameter of the top hat crown template.

15) Place the crown on the brim. Needle all over until it is a matted shape and firmly held in place. You may need to add wisps of grey wool to create a smooth exterior.

16) To make a hat band, roll a piece of black wool between your fingers into a sausage shape that fits all the way around the crown's circumference. Needle into place close to the brim.

17) Take the white rose and push the wire stem through the wool lapel to make a buttonhole. Hide any hanging wire in the jacket and needle gently over the hiding place so that it stays hidden.

Uncle Sam

Stars and stripes forever

You will need

- Needle-felted male figure, made following the instructions for Making a Felted Figure
- White wool, for the trousers, shirt, waistcoat, beard, hair, eyes, teeth, eyebrows and eyelashes
- Red wool, for the stripes on the trousers, bow tie, top hat, lips and stars on the waistcoat
- Blue wool, for the jacket, irises and hat band
- Black wool, for the shoes and pupils
- White and red star-shaped sequins (optional)
- Single size 38 triangle felting needle
- 4-prong needle holder fitted with triangle size 38 needles

1) Add the facial features to the figure. Make eyelashes, eyebrows and hair using white wool.

2) Make the mouth, then needle a white wisp of wool into the centre for the teeth, making sure that the red of the lips shows all around the white.

3) Add a moustache and a pointed beard using white wool.

4) For the waistcoat, arrange a small handful of white wool on the upper torso, front only. Needle from the chin to the waist. To form the lapels, roll a small piece of white wool between your fingers into a sausage shape. Place as a V on the chest and needle gently to keep a raised shape.

5) For the star decoration on the waistcoat, form small wisps of red wool into flat 5-pointed stars. Needle onto the waistcoat. Alternatively, use star-shaped sequins and glue them onto the waistcoat instead.

6) To make a bow tie, roll a small piece of red wool between your fingers into a short sausage shape. Needle flat on the pad. Place at the centre of the neck, making sure it is flush with the beard and needle into place.

7) Take a wisp of white wool and needle over the middle of the bow tie.

8) To make each shoe, wrap a small amount of black wool around the foot. Needle into place.

9) For the trousers, wrap small handfuls of white wool over the lower torso, bottom and legs. Needle into place.

10) To make the stripes, roll a small piece

of red wool between your fingers to a long thin sausage shape. Measure against the leg until the roll is long enough to reach from the waist to the shoe without stretching. Needle into place. Repeat evenly around the trousers.

11) Using the jacket template provided, pull a handful of blue wool into shape. Place it on the pad and needle until matted and firm, turning once. Use the 4-prong needle holder for speed. Wrap around the figure and attach at the shoulders and front.

12) For the sleeves, wrap wool around the arms and needle into place. Add more wisps of wool until satisfied.

13) For the jacket collar, roll a small piece of blue wool between your fingers into a long sausage shape, ensuring it fits the jacket lapel area. Needle the collar to the jacket.

14) To make the hat, fold in a piece of red wool to create a circle. Fit to the top hat brim template provided. Place on the pad and using the 4-prong needle holder, needle until flat, firm and matted.

15) For the crown, roll a larger amount of red wool into a fat slightly stumpy sausage, 5 cm (2 in) long with a diameter that fits the crown template. Place it in the centre of the brim and needle all over until it is a firmly matted piece with the brim attached. Add wisps of red wool to create a smooth exterior.

16) For the hat band, roll a piece of blue wool between your fingers into a sausage shape that fits the hat's circumference. Needle into place close to the brim.

17) Make white wool star shapes as before and needle onto the hat band.

Native American

Add beads and feathers to this lady.

You will need

- Needle-felted female figure, made following the instructions for Making a Felted Figure
- Red wool, for the dress, lips and war paint
- Brown wool, for the irises and moccasins
- Black wool, for the hair, pupils, eyebrows and eyelashes
- White wool, for the teeth, war paint and eyes
- Red ric-rac braid, for the headband
- 1 white feather
- A few beads
- Beading needle
- Cotton
- Glue
- Felting needles
- Single size 38 triangle felting needle
- 4-prong needle holder fitted with triangle size 38 needles

1) Add the facial features to the figure. When making the mouth, take a small piece of red wool and roll it lightly between your fingers. Place on the face, curving the mouth upward and needle firmly into a half moon shape.

2) For the teeth, place a smaller piece of white wool in the middle of the mouth and needle gently, making sure that the red of the lips shows all around the teeth and that she has a big smile.

3) For the hair, take a larger amount of black wool and pull into a rectangle of 36 x 8 cm (14 x 3 in). Centre the rectangle on top of the head and needle a parting down the middle. Secure the right and left sides of the hair to the rest of the head down to the neck.

4) Take the left-hand side of the loose hair and divide into three. Plait (braid) these sections together. Secure to the figure with a wisp of red wool. Repeat on the right side.

5) To make the war paint, needle a wisp of red wool onto the right cheek in a diagonal line. Needle in place. Add a wisp of white wool beneath, then another red strip below that. Repeat on the other side.

6) To make the top half of the dress, wrap a piece of red wool around the upper body to look like a dress top. Needle into place.

7) To make short sleeves, wrap small pieces of red wool around the top of each arm. Needle into place.

8) To make the skirt, pull a large piece of red wool into a rectangle large enough to go around the figure, and long enough to reach

the knees. Place the rectangle on the pad and needle until flat and firm. Wrap around the figure, placing the join at the centre back. Now needle firmly around the waist and gently down the back seam. Add wisps of red wool to hide the seam, and needle gently.

9) To make each mocassin, flatten a piece of brown wool with your fingers. Shape it around the foot. The moccasins are like ankle boots. Needle in place.

10) Thread a beading needle, and stitch beads at random over each moccasin.

11) Thread a string of beads and wrap around the upper arm, stitching into place.

12) Cut a piece of ric-rac braid to fit around the head and stitch in place as a headband.

13) Dip the end of the feather in glue and stick to the side of the headband over the join.

Cowboy

Howdy stranger.

You will need

- Needle-felted male figure, made following the instructions for Making a Felted Figure

- Black wool, for the hat, trousers and pupils

- Red wool, for the shirt, headband and lips

- Blue wool, for the eye and neckerchief

- Brown wool, for the hair, eyebrows, eyelashes, shoes and moustache

- 4 small metal rings

- Small piece of black leather or felt

- Glue

- Single size 38 triangle felting needle

1) Add the facial features to the figure. Add a brown wool moustache. Add brown hair, eyebrows and eyelashes. Use blue wool for the irises.

2) For the trousers, wrap a handful of black wool around the lower torso and all the way down the legs. Add more wool, if needed, Needle into place.

3) For the open-neck shirt, wrap a handful of red wool around the figure's top, leaving a V at the neckline. Wrap small pieces of red wool around the tops of the arms. Needle into place to form short sleeves. For the collar, gently pull a piece of red wool until it's long enough to go around the neck. Needle flat on the pad then attach to the shirt.

4) To make the neckerchief, gently pull a piece of blue wool into a triangle, making sure it's long enough to tie around the neck. Needle flat on the pad, then tie around the neck. Arrange the folds, then needle gently into place.

5) To make each shoe, flatten a piece of brown wool in your fingers, then fold around the foot. Needle into place.

6) For the waistcoat, using the template provided, cut each shape from leather or felt. Stitch the shoulder seams, turn right side out and place on the figure.

7) For the belt, cut the leather into a thin strip to hang just below the waist and so it overlaps slightly.

8) Cut 2 holsters using the template provided. Carefully make 2 slits at the top

of each holster to thread the belt through. Thread the holsters onto the belt, then wrap the belt around the figure starting and finishing at the centre front. Glue the ends of the belt together. Glue 3 metal rings over this join to make a buckle. Position the holsters at each side of the waist.

9) To make the hat, shape a piece of black wool into a circle by folding the edges inward. Match this against the template provided for the hat brim and needle flat on the pad until firm. For the crown, take a clump of black wool and fold into a smaller circle using the template provided as a guideline. Needle on the pad until firm and matted and the depth is 2 cm (¾ in). Needle the brim and crown together on the pad before needling onto the head.

10) For the hat band, roll a piece of red wool

between your fingers into a sausage shape that fits around the crown circumference. Wrap around the hat then through a metal ring. Needle into place close to the brim with a ring at the centre front.

The Sailor

All the nice girls love a sailor.

You will need

- Needle-felted male figure, made following the instructions for Making a Felted Figure

- White wool, for the sailor suit, hat, teeth and eyes

- Black wool, for the hair, beard, shoes, eyelashes, eyebrows and neckerchief

- Brown wool, for the irises

- Red wool, for the lips

- Grey wool, for the buckle

- Single size 38 triangle felting needle

1) Add the facial features to the figure. This character has a toothy grin. For the mouth, take a small piece of red wool and roll it between your fingers. Make a half-moon shape and needle this on to the face at a slight angle.

2) For the teeth, take a wisp of white wool, roll it between your fingers and place it in the middle of the half-moon mouth. Needle into place, making sure the red lips show all around.

3) Make a black wool beard, eyebrows and eyelashes.

4) Use brown wool for the irises.

5) For the trousers, take a handful of white wool, needle it around the lower torso and all the way down the legs. Build up the volume of white wool on the lower legs to make a bell-bottom trouser leg.

6) For the shirt, take some white wool and needle it around the upper torso leaving a V at the neckline. Take small pieces of white wool and wrap around the arms. Needle into place to create long sleeves.

7) For the collar, measure around the neck. Take a piece of white wool to the length of the measurement and needle it flat on the pad. Attach it to the shirt.

8) To make the neckerchief, roll a piece of black wool between your fingers until it's long enough to go all the way around the neck and finish at the waist. Wrap around the neck, under the collar. Cross it over the chest. Take a wisp of black wool and wrap around the crossover point. Needle gently into place.

9) To make the belt, roll a piece of white wool between your fingers into a sausage shape that will fit around the waist. Flatten it slightly on the pad before wrapping around the figure. Start and finish at the centre of the waist. Needle gently into place.

10) For the belt buckle, roll a small piece of grey wool into a thin sausage. Needle into a square over the centre join.

11) To make each shoe, take a piece of black wool and flatten it, then fold it around the foot. Needle into place.

12) For the sailor's hat, take a handful of white wool and fold the corners in to create a circle. Needle on the pad to make a hat shape. Use the template provided as a guide to size and shape. As each figure is individual, make sure it's the right size for your figure's head before you needle it in place. It needs to be very firm and at least 1 cm (3/8 in) deep. Attach to the man's head by needling until secure.

The Pirate

Yo ho ho and a bottle of rum.

You will need

- Needle-felted male figure, made following the instructions for Making a Felted Figure

- Black wool, for the hair, eyelashes, moustache, pupils, beard and boots

- Red wool, for the lips, neckerchief and trousers

- White wool, for the shirt and eyes

- Brown wool, for the tricorn hat and wooden wrist

- Blue wool, for the irises

- Yellow wool, for the belt

- A small hook

- Single size 38 triangle felting needle

- Toy plastic knife

- Black leather or felt, for the waistcoat

- Sewing needle and thread

1) Add the facial features to the figure. Use blue wool for the irises. The eyebrows, eyelashes and long hair are black.

2) For the moustache, take a piece of black wool and roll it in your fingers into a short fat sausage. For the beard, shape a smaller piece of black wool into a triangle and place under the bottom lip. Needle into place.

3) For the trousers, take a handful of red wool, wrap it around the lower torso and halfway down the legs. Needle into place.

4) For the shirt, wrap a piece of white wool around the upper torso to make a vest, leaving a V at the neckline. Needle into place.

5) For the hook hand, bend the left hand back on itself so it is folded up against the wrist and push the screw end of the hook into the wool until hidden. Position the hook where the hand should be and glue into place. When the glue is dry, needle around the base of the hook and wrist with brown wool to create the wooden stump.

6) For the long blousy sleeves, wrap small pieces of white wool around the arms. Needle into place. Build up the lower end of the sleeves to give a bloused appearance. Make sure that the hook faces inward.

7) For the collar, fit a piece of white wool around the neck to check for length. Needle flat on the pad into a collar shape, then attach to the shirt.

8) To make the neckerchief, roll a small piece of red wool between your fingers until it's long enough to go all the way around the neck when tied in a knot. Wrap around the neck and tie to the side. Needle gently into place.

9) For the belt, roll a piece of yellow wool between your fingers to a sausage shape that fits around the figure's waist. Flatten it slightly on the pad before wrapping around the figure. Needle gently into place. Needle small wisps of yellow wool to hide the join.

10) For each boot, take a piece of black wool and flatten it on the pad, then fold it around the foot and lower leg. Add more wool as necessary. Needle into place. For the turned down cuff, roll a piece of black wool into a fat sausage that fits around the top of the boot. Flatten on the pad until firm, turning once. Needle into place.

11) For the hat brim, take a handful of brown wool and fold into a circle. Needle on the pad until it matches the template provided for the Outback Explorer's hat. As each figure is individual, make sure it is the right size for your figure's head.

12) For the crown, fold some brown wool into a smaller round circle, using the template provided. Needle firmly. The depth of this piece is 2 cm (¾ in). Now needle the brim and crown together. The pirate wears a tricorn hat. The achieve this look, mark the brim at three equal points, then lift the brim at each in turn and attach to the crown by needling firmly. Place on the head with one point at the front, needle firmly into place.

13) If you have a toy knife, push it in his belt.

14) For the waistcoat, cut 1 shape from leather or felt using the template provided. Stitch along the shoulder seams, turn right side out and place on the figure.

The Gangster

You looking at me wise guy?

You will need

- Needle-felted male figure, made following the instructions for Making a Felted Figure

- Grey wool, for the suit

- Black wool, for the shirt, shoes, hat and pupils

- Brown wool, for the eyelashes, eyebrows and hair

- White wool, for the teeth, eyes, tie and hat band

- Red wool, for the lips

- Blue wool, for the irises

- Small paper flower

- Small toy plastic gun

- Single size 38 triangle felting needle

- 4-prong needle holder fitted with triangle size 38 needles

1) Add the facial features to the figure. Use blue wool for the irises. Use brown wool for the hair, eyelashes and eyebrows.

2) This figure has an angry face. To create the expression, place the edge of your eyebrow closer to the top of the eye and the nose.

3) For the scowling mouth, roll and tease a small piece of red wool into the shape of a speech bubble, then needle gently onto the face under the nose.

4) For the teeth, form a smaller piece of white wool into the same shape and needle into the centre of the red mouth leaving the red lips visible all around. This gives your figure a sneering expression.

5) For the trousers, wrap a handful of grey wool around the lower torso and each leg. Needle into place.

6) For each shoe, wrap a small piece of black wool around the foot. Add more wisps, if needed, and needle until satisfied.

7) For the shirt front, needle a piece of black wool onto the chest from the chin to the waist.

8) For the shirt collar, roll a smaller amount of black wool into a sausage shape that fits around the neck. Place on the pad and needle into a flat collar (use the template provided). Needle the collar to the shirt.

9) For the tie, roll a small piece of white wool between your fingers into a small ball. Place at the centre of the neck on the shirt to make a knot for a tie. Roll another piece

of white wool into a thin strip, and arrange vertically down the chest. Needle the tie into place.

10) Take a handful of grey wool, place on the pad and pull into the shape of a jacket. (Use the template provided). Needle the wool using the 4-prong needle holder until matted and firm, turning once. Wrap around the figure and attach at the shoulders, front and back.

11) Wrap more wool around the arms and needle the sleeves into place. Add more wisps of wool until satisfied.

12) Make the jacket collar, by pulling some grey wool into shape, using the template provided and needling flat on the pad. Needle the collar gently to the jacket.

13) For the hat, shape a piece of black wool into a circle, using the template provided. Needle until firm. For the crown, take some black wool and fold into a circle using the template provided. Needle firmly to a depth of 2 cm (¾ in).

14) For the hat band, roll a piece of white wool between your fingers into a sausage shape that fits the crown circumference. Needle into place close to the brim. Now needle both the brim and crown together before needling onto the head.

15) Take the rose, pierce the lapel with the wire stem and pull through to give the figure a buttonhole. Hide any leftover wire in the wool.

16) Place the small plastic gun in the gangster's hands.

The Boxer

Float like a butterfly, sting like a bee.

You will need

- Needle-felted male figure, made following the instructions for Making a Felted Figure

- Black wool, for the eyelashes, eyebrows, hair and shoe laces

- White wool, for the teeth, eyes and shorts

- Red wool, for the lips, boxing gloves and boots

- Mid-brown wool, for the irises

- Toy belt

- Glue

- Single size 38 triangle felting needle

1) Add the facial features to the figure. Use mid-brown wool for the irises and black wool for hair, eyebrows and eyelashes.

2) This character has a toothy grin. Roll a small piece of red wool between your fingers. Form into a half-moon shape and needle this onto the face at a slight angle.

3) For the teeth, roll a wisp of white wool between your fingers and place in the middle of the half-moon mouth. Needle into place making sure the red of the lips show all around.

4) For the shorts, needle a handful of white wool around the lower torso and half way down the thighs.

5) For each boot, wrap a piece of red wool. around the foot and halfway up the leg. Add more wisps of wool, if needed and needle, until satisfied.

6) For the boot laces, roll a small piece of black wool between your fingers to make a thin sausage shape. Needle onto the front of the boot, criss-crossing over, to bring the laces all the way up the boot.

7) For the padded boxing gloves, wrap a piece of red wool around the hand, leaving some wool hanging over. Roll this wool up, finishing halfway down the hand to give the impression of boxing gloves. Needle firmly into place.

8) Glue the belt around the waist

Exotic Dancer

Think Arabian nights.

You will need

- Needle-felted female figure, made following the instructions for Making a Felted Figure
- Red wool, for the bikini top, pants, soles of sandals and lips
- White wool, for the eyes
- Brown wool, for the irises
- Black wool for the hair, eyebrows and eyeliner
- Small crystal, for the belly button
- Three different types of thin braid in red, gold and yellow
- A small piece of red diaphanous material, to match the braid
- Glue
- Sewing needle and red thread
- Single size 38 triangle felting needle

1) Add the facial features to your figure. Use black wool to create thin eyebrows and eyeliner. When lining the eyes, make your roll of wool slightly thicker than usual and use it to clearly define the eye area to give the impression of heavy make-up.

2) Make the hair black and shoulder length.

3) For the bikini top, take a piece of red wool and position over the bust. Needle into place. Wrap the red and gold braid just under the bust and needle the wool over the top to hold it in place.

4) To make the pants, wrap a piece of red wool around the figure's hips. Needle firmly into place.

5) For the sole of the shoe, shape a small piece of red wool to fit the underside of the foot. Make 2. Do not attach it just yet.

6) Wrap a length of gold braid around the foot as if it is the strap of a sandal. Cut to size and position with the join under the foot. Place the red sole over the join and needle both firmly in place.

7) For the skirt, measure and cut a rectangle of diaphanous material that is long enough to go from the hips to the feet, and wide enough to fit around the figure. With the sewing needle and thread, stitch a thin braid around two short and one long edges. Stitch the plain edge around the hips, leaving a gap at the front. Cover the 'waistband' with a decorative braid.

8) For the shawl, cut a strip of material and stitch a decorative braid all around the edge. Drape around the arms.

9) String a small piece of braid across the forehead, stitching the ends into place. Needle wisps of black wool over the ends until they are hidden.

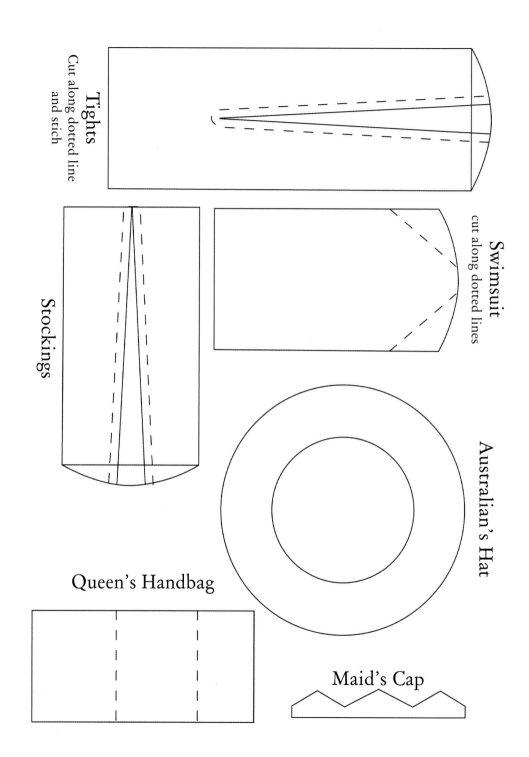

Templates

Tights
Cut along dotted line and stich

Swimsuit
cut along dotted lines

Stockings

Australian's Hat

Queen's Handbag

Maid's Cap

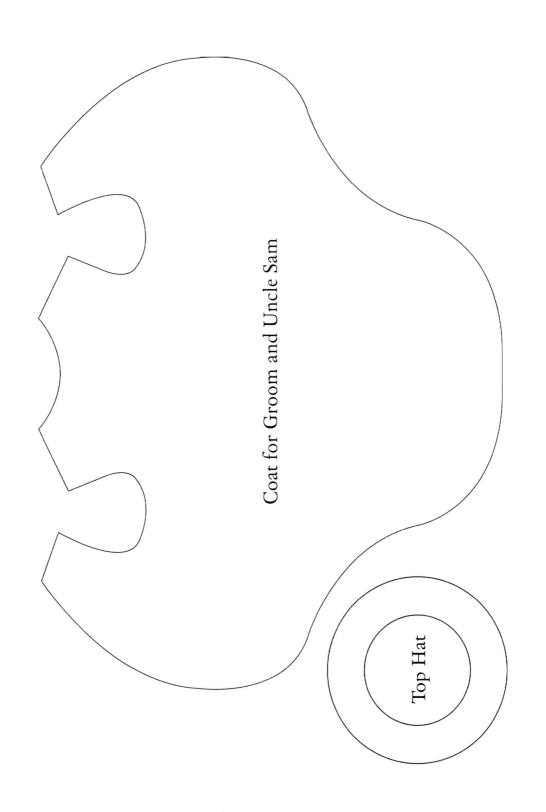

Coat for Groom and Uncle Sam

Top Hat

Gangster's Hat

Jacket for Prince Philip and Gangster

Maid's Apron

Gather along here

Sailor's Hat

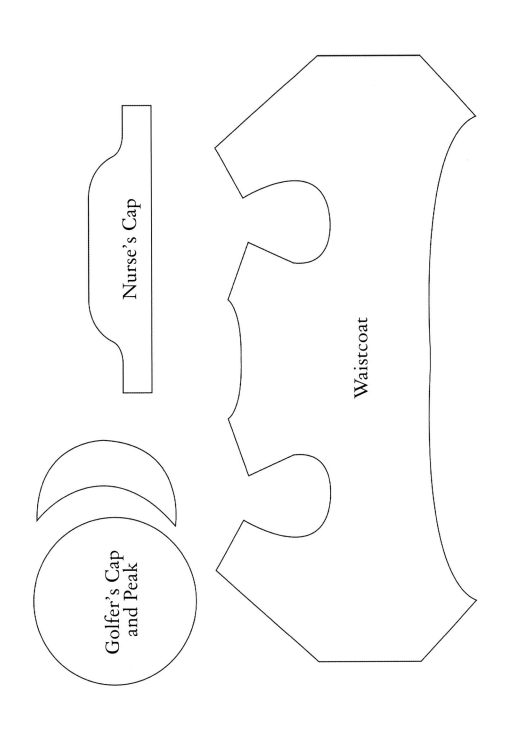

Nurse's Cap

Waistcoat

Golfer's Cap and Peak

First published in 2015 by
New Holland Publishers Pty Ltd
London • Sydney • Auckland

The Chandlery Unit 009 50 Westminster Bridge Road
    London SE1 7QY United Kingdom
1/66 Gibbes Street Chatswood NSW 2067 Australia
218 Lake Road Northcote Auckland New Zealand

www.newhollandpublishers.com

A record of this book is held at the British Library and the National Library of Australia.

ISBN 9781742575773

Managing Director: Fiona Schultz
Publisher: Diane Ward
Editor: Simona Hill
Designer: Andrew Quinlan
Photographer: Natalie Hunfalvay
Production Director: Olga Dementiev
Printer: Toppan Leefung Printing Ltd

10 9 8 7 6 5 4 3 2 1

Keep up with New Holland Publishers on Facebook
www.facebook.com/NewHollandPublishers

UK £12.99